Neoliberalism, Education, and Terrorism

Neoliberalism, Education, and Terrorism
Contemporary Dialogues

Jeffrey R. Di Leo, Henry A. Giroux,
Sophia A. McClennen, and
Kenneth J. Saltman

Taylor & Francis Group
LONDON AND NEW YORK

First published 2013 by Paradigm Publishers

Published 2016 by Routledge
2 Park Square, Milton Park, Abingdon, Oxon OX14 4RN
711 Third Avenue, New York, NY 10017, USA

Routledge is an imprint of the Taylor & Francis Group, an informa business

Copyright © 2013, Taylor & Francis.

All rights reserved. No part of this book may be reprinted or reproduced or utilised in any form or by any electronic, mechanical, or other means, now known or hereafter invented, including photocopying and recording, or in any information storage or retrieval system, without permission in writing from the publishers.

Notice:
Product or corporate names may be trademarks or registered trademarks, and are used only for identification and explanation without intent to infringe.

Library of Congress Cataloging-in-Publication Data
Di Leo, Jeffrey R. author.
Neoliberalism, education, and terrorism : contemporary dialogues / by Jeffrey R. Di Leo, Henry A. Giroux, Sophia McClennen, and Kenneth J. Saltman.
  pages cm
  Includes index.
  ISBN 978-1-61205-039-3 (hardcover : alk. paper)
  1. Education—Political aspects—United States. 2. Neoliberalism—United States. 3. Terrorism—United States—Psychological aspects. I. Giroux, Henry A. author. II. McClennen, Sophia A. author. III. Saltman, Kenneth J., 1969– author. IV. Title.
  LC89.D525   2012
  379—dc23

                                                                    2012018914

ISBN 13 : 978-1-61205-039-3 (hbk)
ISBN 13 : 978-1-61205-040-9 (pbk)

Contents

Acknowledgments	vii
Introduction: Neoliberalism, Education, Terrorism—*Jeffrey R. Di Leo, Henry A. Giroux, Sophia A. McClennen, and Kenneth J. Saltman*	1
1 Militarizing Higher Education, Neoliberalism's Culture of Depravity, and Democracy's Demise after 9/11—*Henry A. Giroux*	36
2 Venture Philanthropy and the Neoliberal Assault on Public Education—*Kenneth J. Saltman*	67
3 Neoliberalism as Terrorism; or, State of Disaster Exceptionalism—*Sophia A. McClennen*	94
4 On Academic Terrorism: Neoliberalism, Higher Education, and the Politics of Emotion—*Jeffrey R. Di Leo*	115
Conclusion: Twelve Theses on Education's Future in the Age of Neoliberalism and Terrorism—*Jeffrey R. Di Leo, Henry A. Giroux, Sophia A. McClennen, and Kenneth J. Saltman*	135
Notes	143
Index	163
About the Authors	173

Acknowledgments

We would like to thank Dean Birkenkamp and Jason Barry of Paradigm Publishers for their encouragement and support of this project. A note of appreciation also goes out to Keri Farnsworth for her editorial assistance and work on the index.

Introduction: Neoliberalism, Education, Terrorism

Jeffrey R. Di Leo, Henry A. Giroux,
Sophia A. McClennen, and Kenneth J. Saltman

> The events and aftermath of September 11, 2001, have underscored the need for the nation to strengthen and enhance American knowledge of international relations, world regions, and foreign languages. Homeland security and effective United States engagement abroad depend upon an increased number of Americans who have received such training and are willing to serve their nation.
> —*College Access and Opportunity Act of 2005*
> *(Sec 601 of HR 609)*[1]

The core idea of this book is that educational policy today has been greatly shaped by two complementary practices: neoliberalism and terrorism. Neoliberalism, otherwise known as extreme free-market capitalism, has influenced the funding of higher education while simultaneously reducing the state's commitment to providing citizens with basic services. The advent of the post-9/11 era of terrorism has brought with it increased militarization, rampant xenophobia, a culture of fear, and a massive national debt. These forces have worked together to create a series of practices and beliefs that have had dire effects for the possibilities of progressive education committed to offering young citizens the means through which to actively participate in democracy.

The goal of this book, then, is to provide the perspective of four scholars who have worked on this topic from different, yet complementary, angles. One of our shared beliefs is that the first step in confronting these changes is to be aware of the ways that neoliberalism and terrorism operate in current education practices. Neoliberal administrative policies have had a largely negative impact on the quality of education in the United States; couple these with policies stemming from the war on terror in the wake of the terror attacks of September 11, 2001, and the immediate future of education and democratic culture appears quite reactionary and dire. Thus, while much of what we describe in the following pages might appear gloomy and depressing, particularly for those who believe in the progressive and transformative powers of education, this book is ultimately about thinking through ways to imagine other solutions to the current education crisis that do not trap us in the current status quo.

The aim of this project is to introduce some of the problems resulting from the coming together of neoliberalism, education, and terrorism—and to suggest ways to build a future for education and democratic culture that avoid them. But before we introduce the critical ideas central to the book, first a word about how it was written. We worked together on both the introduction and the conclusion and then each contributed one of the main chapters. Readers will note that in the collectively written pieces we avoided an urge to create a unified voice, allowing our different writing styles to operate collaboratively. We would like you to regard what follows *dialogically*—or simply think of it as a contemporary form of *dialogue*. Our dialogue is *dialogic* because we are familiar with and admirers of each other's writing, meaning that oftentimes you can hear different voices or echoes of the other in individual lines. This is evident in both the collaborative parts of the book—the introduction and conclusion—as well as in the individual contributions. At times you will notice the voice transitions, whereas at other times you may not. We hope that they will not distract you from our project.

In the chapter that follows here we introduce some of the current points of connection among neoliberalism, education, and terrorism. We provide background to many of the key issues that we analyze in the following chapters. Our goal in the introduction is to explain how the variety of forces influencing education today—economic policy, state policy, the war on terror, and the rise of right-wing fundamentalisms, and so on—cannot be understood as separate forces, but must be seen as operating in collusion. The essays that follow the introduction take on four unique but related points of entry on our topic.

In "Militarizing Higher Education, Neoliberalism's Culture of Depravity, and Democracy's Demise after 9/11," Henry Giroux argues that if higher education is to come to grips with the multilayered pathologies produced by neoliberalism and its formative culture of cruelty and militarization of everyday life, students, faculty, and others will have to rethink both the space of the university as a democratic public sphere and the global spaces and public sites in which intellectuals, educators, students, artists, labor unions, and other social actors and movements can form transnational alliances to oppose the death-dealing ideology of militarization and its effects on the world. Kenneth J. Saltman's "Venture Philanthropy and the Neoliberal Assault on Public Education" shows how the new venture philanthropy shares the same neoliberal logic ("education as enforcement") animating the ongoing militarization and corporatization of schools and calls instead for a public and democratic conception of educational obligation. "Neoliberalism as Terrorism; or, State of Disaster Exceptionalism" by Sophia McClennen focuses on the way that the current educational structure has brought with it a particular worldview that makes it extremely difficult to understand the connections between state practices, the new neoliberal imperialism, ideas about how human life is valued, and geopolitical prejudices. And Jeffrey R. Di Leo's "On

Academic Terrorism" argues that the primary emotional effect of neoliberalism in education is *fear*, and that the promotion of neoliberal academic policies is itself a type of terrorism, namely, *academic* terrorism. We conclude by collaboratively postulating some theses regarding the future of education under the dual shadows of neoliberalism and terrorism.

It is our belief that educators need to be aware of and work out the meaning and implications of neoliberalism and terrorism. Terrorism and neoliberalism work in connection with each other in the context of educational policy and practice. Seeing the results of this threatening nexus is the first step in working toward providing a better educational future for everyone.

The Denial of Politics

Neoliberalism, the discourse on terrorism, and contemporary educational policy all share a *denial of politics*, a redistributive economic dimension, and a tendency against democratic culture and toward fundamentalist thought. As an economic doctrine neoliberalism calls for the privatization of public goods and services, deregulation of state controls over capital, allowance of foreign direct investment, and financialization. In practice, neoliberal economic policy expands state spending on the punitive and repressive roles of the state while decreasing the caregiving roles of the state.

The United States is well on the way to privatizing its public education system through chartering, vouchers, contracting, and applying market-based language and logic to educational policy and practice. Both political parties have accepted a number of organizing neoliberal values including treating public schooling as primarily workforce and consumer preparation rather than as primarily a public good dedicated to preparing citizens for collective self-governance. They have also rejected equal distribution of educational resources and desegregation in favor of a market-based model of "competition" and "choice" among schools, districts, and states for resources made scarce rather than made available based on need. This, as we shall see, is the case with No Child Left Behind (NCLB), Race to the Top, and Urban Portfolio Districts.

There are two primary motivations behind the neoliberal assault on public education. First there is a profit motive. For more than a decade the corporate sector has seen the roughly $600 billion per year spent on education in the United States as a valuable source of revenue, comparing the investment opportunities to military contracting and agriculture.[2] Education is big business as evidenced by the multi-billion dollar testing and textbook publishing industries, for-profit management of schools, and educational services such as contracting and tutoring.[3]

The Educational Management Organization (EMO) focuses on managing schools for profit; 94 percent of EMOs are charter schools. As of 2008–2009, at least 95 EMOs were operating in 31 states, with 339,222 students and at least 733 schools and with nearly 80 percent of students in schools managed by the 16 largest EMOs. Major companies include Edison Learning (62 schools), The Leona Group (67 schools), National Heritage Academies (57), White Hat Management (51), Imagine Schools, Inc. (76), Academica (54), the rapidly growing virtual online school company K12 (24), and Mosaica (33).[4] The largest EMO in terms of number of students, The Edison Schools (now Edison Learning), has been beset by numerous financial and accountability scandals that have less to do with corrupt individuals than with the impositions of privatization and the social costs of public deregulation.

Major privatization initiatives also include market-based voucher schemes allowed by the U.S. Supreme Court in 2002 (Zelman *v.* Harris-Simmons) and implemented by the U.S. Congress in Washington, DC, and in the gulf region following hurricane Katrina.[5] States such as Wisconsin used the financial crisis of 2008 and state budget crises that followed to expand vouchers and charters drastically while cutting educational spending on traditional public schools and also limiting local taxes used for public schools while cutting corporate taxes. Education conglomerate companies, such as junk-bond felon Michael Milken's Knowledge Universe, aim to amass a number of different education companies. These conglomerate companies hold a variety of for-profit educational enterprises, including test publishing; textbook publishing; tutoring services; curriculum consultancies; educational software development, publication, and sales; toy making; and other companies.[6]

In the United States, the Elementary and Secondary Education Act (No Child Left Behind) has fostered privatization by investing billions of public dollars in the charter school movement, which is pushing privatization with more than three-quarters of new for-profits being opened as charters. NCLB also requires high-stakes testing, accountability, and remediation measures that shift resources away from public school control and into control by test and textbook publishing corporations and for-profit remediation companies. As well, NCLB's Supplemental Educational Services (SES) provision required for-profit remediation of low scores rather than investment in public schools needing help.

For-profit EMOs are only one part of the private takeover of schools themselves. Nonprofit charters are premised on injecting a healthy dose of "market competition" into schooling, forcing schools to compete against each other for students and letting those that do not raise scores go out of business. Despite the business rhetoric of competition, since their inception charters have relied disproportionately on grants and philanthropic donations (the Gates Foundation poured billions into charters) and now increasingly government incentives and one-time payouts.

The major academic national studies of charters find that, on the whole, they do worse than traditional public schools in traditional measures of student achievement.[7] It is important to realize that in the past decade charters have gotten unending political support from the zealous, organized, and richly funded charter movement, which includes national and state charter lobbying groups such as state charter school associations and Washington think tanks like Fordham, AEI, Hoover, and Heritage. They also receive financial support from the so-called "venture philanthropies"[8] especially the Gates and Broad Foundations, the New Schools Venture Fund, and the Charter School Growth Fund, all of which aim to replace public schooling with a national "market" in education.

Despite starting as a grassroots movement for innovative, independent, and alternative school models, the now dominant corporate model of the "venture philanthropists" (neoliberal educational philanthropy such as Gates, Broad, and Walton that sees public education as a private market) has emphasized replicating traditional school models and rigid approaches to learning that stand to create not innovation but rather homogeneous "McEducation." The instability and unsustainability of charters comes in part from the fact that the extra money from these philanthropies and from the government can and will dry up. When this happens, charters will eventually go out of business, but not before doing all they can to cut costs to survive. Such cost-cutting has historically included displacing and underpaying local experienced teachers; hiring inexperienced teachers and burning them out while their salaries are low; using inexpensive and inexperienced Teach for America teachers, uncertified teachers, or relying on alternative certification[9]; union-busting; manipulating test scores; importing low-wage teachers from overseas; counseling or pushing out special needs students and English language learners to raise test scores; and contracting the running of schools to for-profit management companies.

Charters are often public in name but not in practice. Charters shift governance to unelected councils dominated by business people who redistribute decisions about schools away from public community control. They subcontract to private for-profit companies that drain public funds and can maintain financial secrecy away from public oversight. They introduce new educational inequalities under the guise of freedom of choice as they favor those citizens with the most money, social networks, and cultural savvy to game the school selection process. Charters also drain public resources as schools compete with each other to draw parents by spending money on private public relations and advertising that could be spent on teachers, books, and schools. Charters imagine students economically as workers and consumers, and consequently they overemphasize high-stakes tests, which in turn pushes schools to treat knowledge as something that students consume and regurgitate rather than foster the kind of public education that prepares students to think critically about the world they inhabit and to learn to act as citizens with others to change that world for the better. Charters fail to address the problems of racial segregation and White flight, becoming complicit with the abandonment of the democratic aspirations of the civil rights movement. As the Democratic party steals the educational reform agenda from the Republicans, the political Right is organizing to support charters in the short run in order to later declare them as a failed experiment and set the stage for radically expanded educational privatization. That is, charters set the stage for future school privatizations by for-profit companies by being subject to closure.

The second motive for the neoliberal assault on public education is ideological. Advocates of neoliberal education are true believers that public education ought to be modeled on the necessarily efficient private sector. The public sector in this view is necessarily bureaucratically encumbered and inefficient. As an ideology neoliberalism promotes the social world as a collection of atomistic individuals, social Darwinian rational economic actors. The neoliberal TINA (an acronym for "there is no alternative" . . . to the market) thesis promotes what might be called an anti-politics by suggesting that alternative political ideologies are impossible and the only role for politics is to manage markets. Hence in education administrative and leadership concerns are framed through private sector models while pedagogy is framed as delivery of neutral apolitical content.

Privatization advocates have made up their minds that public education has failed. And the declaration of a failed public system is part of the ideological core of the privatization agenda. It is part of a series of interconnected business metaphors wrongly applied to public schooling. These metaphors include choice, monopoly, competition, consumers, and accountability that frame public schooling as a private business. The educational policy debates are now trapped in this frame, making it difficult to assert crucial democratic educational values such as equality, fairness, justice, care, intellect, and the public good, to name a few.

It is a mistake to think that school privatization and neoliberal education reform are generally Republican or Democratic party issues. Both candidates in the 2008 presidential election spoke of the need to inject competition and choice into the education system. In the fall of 2009, the American Enterprise Institute, which is a leading pro-privatization think tank with a Republican party orientation, teamed up with the Center for American Progress, led by Clinton's Chief of Staff and Obama's transition head John Podesta, to issue a report called "Leaders and Laggards: A State-by-State Report on Educational Innovation." The report was finalized so that each state could know where it stood in relation to the desired reforms of Race to the Top, which follows much the same rationale of NCLB. Race to the Top dangles money in front of states to enjoin them to expand charter schools, ties teacher evaluation and merit pay systems to standardized test scores (thereby undermining critical and public forms of teaching and learning), and encourages local districts to dismiss entire staffs of thousands of "failing" schools. Race to the Top was designed by people from the Gates Foundation and follows the logic of venture philanthropy, which imagines school reform as akin to venture capital in the tech sector. Private money in the venture philanthropy view ought to be "leveraged" in order to influence public spending in line with the agenda from the top. Race to the Top leverages federal money to create a disproportionate influence at the state and local level to achieve the same aims as venture philanthropy—especially privatization and positivist reforms such as value-added assessment to link teacher pay, teacher education, and educational value strictly to standardized testing.[10] Although both political parties see education as business, the difference is that the Democratic party sees privatization strategies as a tool for public school improvement. The thinking here is similar to that of the health-care debates. A big dose of private sector competition should be injected into the public system, and the public schools should be forced to compete with private providers in the form of charters. For the political far Right, the public system has failed, and charters are an interim measure on the road to ending public education and replacing it with publicly funded private schooling. What the advocates for charters who want to strengthen public education do not seem to realize is that once traditional public schools are transformed into charters, they are easy to close and replace with private providers. The push for privatization is based not in evidence but rather in ideology and profit-seeking.

Creative Destruction

In 2004, Bill Gates, who has championed charter schools far more aggressively than anyone, appeared before the National Governors Association and gave a speech, a version of which was reprinted in multiple newspaper op-ed columns. Gates stated, "Our high schools are obsolete. By obsolete, I don't just mean that they're broken, flawed or under-funded, although I could not argue with any of those descriptions. What I mean is that … even when they work exactly as designed, our high schools cannot teach our kids what they need to know…. This is an economic disaster," he said, and one that is ruining children's lives and "is offensive to our values."[11]

Likewise, Pete DuPont of the Lynde and Harry F. Bradley Foundation (a major funder of voucher projects) described the public school system as "awful," the worst thing the government does in America, and as "collectivism" that could be remedied by creating a market in education, and by treating students and parents as consumers of private education. Similarly, Bruno Manno, who has served on the board of Fordham Institute and as a senior associate at the Casey Foundation, wrote in the Hoover Institution–published *Primer on America's Schools* that, "the present school enterprise is not just doing poorly, but is incapable of doing much better because it's intellectually misguided, ideologically wrongheaded, and organizationally dysfunctional."[12]

Despite the frequently heard claims about evidence-based reforms, the goal of neoliberal education is not to improve public education. The goal is to destroy public education and to replace it with a privatized national system of schools competing for scarce public dollars, regularly going out of business and allowing other profit-seekers to try their hand at running schools for profit. If the concentrated ownership characteristic of the EMO industry is any indication, the trend will be toward large corporate consolidation of for-profit school management companies. The privatization advocates call this system of opening privatized schools and closing public schools "creative destruction" or "churn" and make little secret of the long-term vision. For example, Andrew Smarick of the Fordham Foundation and the American Enterprise Institute criticizes the Obama administration's emphasis on school turnarounds and explains that the problem with turnarounds is that they do not readily do what charters set the stage for: closing public schools. He writes that,

> The beginning of the solution is establishing a clear process for closing schools. The simplest and best way to put this into operation is the charter model. Each school, in conjunction with the state or district, would develop a five-year contract with performance measures. Consistent failure to meet goals in key areas would result in closure.... Chartering has demonstrated clearly that the ingredients of healthy, orderly

churn [creative destruction] can be brought to bear on public education.¹³

Natural and human-made disasters are being used to implement school privatization policies that could not be put in place through standard political means. Hurricane Katrina was used to put in place pre-formulated plans for no-bid contracting, to expand turnaround consulting, to create the largest experiment in vouchers to date, to require data reporting from the public sector to be used by the private sector, and most significantly to create the largest and most aggressive experiment in dismantling an entire public school district, firing all the teachers, concentrating control over hiring of teachers and administrators under a single CEO, and replacing the former public district with a largely privatized network of charter schools.¹⁴

What was afoot in the post-Katrina Gulf Coast needs to be understood as part of a broader trend to declare educational institutions as "failed" or as "disaster areas" to justify radical unproven experiments—specifically radical experiments with a business approach to school reform. Rather than seeing such approaches as a marginal phenomenon, we ought to understand this as a dominant trend. The declaration of disaster as a reason for selling off public schools to private companies is found not just in the Gulf Coast but also is at the core of Arne Duncan's corporate-led Chicago school reform "Renaissance 2010." Renaissance 2010 closes 60 schools and opens 100 privatized, de-unionized charters. As well, the educational reconstruction in post-invasion Iraq attempted to install charter schools there with multi-million dollar profits for educational contractor Creative Associates International Incorporated. NCLB also acted aggressively to push charter schools and required extensive use of for-profit Special Educational Service contractors, as well as put in place Adequate Yearly Progress requirements for continual test-based increases that are designed to declare public schools as failed and ripe for closure and privatization in the future.

The Urban Portfolio Model of school reform brings together multiple aspects of neoliberal privatization with creative destruction. It has been implemented by Chicago, New York, Washington, DC, and New Orleans and aggressively promoted by Paul T. Hill at the Center on Reinventing Public Education (CRPE) at the University of Washington. Hill was centrally involved through the Urban Institute in promoting a post-Katrina New Orleans public school policy that involved refusing to rebuild the New Orleans public schools and putting in place the largest educational privatization experiment in U.S. history. The urban portfolio approach draws on the metaphor of stock investment. The district superintendent is imagined as a stock investor who has a portfolio of investments (schools). The superintendent creates a portfolio of contractors and subsequently holds the investments that "perform" (in terms of student achievement) and ends the contracts (or sells) those investments that don't perform. The approach merges four radical corporate restructuring ideas:[15] (1) decentralization, (2) charter school expansion, (3) school closures with charter replacements, and (4) accountability, largely through testing.[16] The portfolio district is imagined as a circuit of continuous improvement in which schools are assessed on the basis of test scores. If scores are low, schools are subject to possible closure (or mass firings) and to being reopened as charters. If the charters subsequently fail to show desired improvements, they in turn are subject to possible closure and replacement by still other contractors. The portfolio district concept puts into place what has been increasingly discussed in educational policy literature as market-based creative destruction or churn.[17] Despite rhetoric across the political spectrum of the need for "evidence-based" reform, the urban portfolio model and its constituent reforms are not backed by any scholarly empirically based, peer-reviewed evidence. And according to Hill and the CRPE, although standardized test scores should be the basis for privatizing public schools, the complexity of the reform renders standardized tests a dubious means of measuring the success of those privatized schools. Instead, incredibly, privatization itself would be a measure of successful implementation of the reform.[18]

While post-Katrina New Orleans was a model for radical neoliberal restructuring that followed an elaborate plan for refusing to rebuild public schools, firing teachers, smashing unions, and putting in place charters and vouchers that were otherwise unachievable, the attacks and privatizations of public education in Wisconsin by Governor Walker, in New Jersey by Governor Christie, as well as in Indiana and in Michigan in 2011 followed an established game plan.[19] Anticipating the bursting of the housing bubble and the economic downturn of 2008, Connecticut's right-wing Yankee Institute put an ad in the *Heartland School News* in 2005: when the real estate bubble bursts and public education "costs soar relative to home values" in rich communities, wrote Executive Director Lewis Andrews, "savvy reformers will be prepared to make the case for school vouchers in all communities."

Despite the profoundly political dimensions to neoliberal educational restructuring, these reforms that redistribute wealth and public resources upward, shift governance and control to financial elites, and run counter to critical pedagogical values and public interest are nonetheless put forward as if they are about efficient delivery of a neutral service. Neoliberal education's denial of politics is defined by positivist rationality. Allegedly neutral units of knowledge that must be quantifiably measurable (curriculum) are delivered to the student by the teacher. In this resurgent positivism the crucial critical questions about the relationship between knowledge-making and power are denied while the purpose of teaching and learning is framed explicitly toward capitalist ends. In the new market positivism used to justify privatization, crucial questions about whose knowledge matters, who creates the test questions, and how particular claims to truth secure particular kinds of social authority are denied. Knowledge is not subject to being produced by dialogic exchange in this view. Rather it is something that comes from the experts who know and who are elsewhere. This knowledge must be enforced, consumed, measured, and then exchanged for future educational advancement toward the end of competing for scarce economic opportunities.

Ultimately the promise of neoliberal education is the promise to compete for inclusion in consumer capitalism. Such a view has no way of addressing the ways that unlimited growth of markets tends toward the production of vast human social and environmental waste. Neoliberal education is education as enforcement, rather than education as access to and engagement with a democratic public sphere. Dialogue and debate are forsaken in favor of the acquisition of "neutral" facts and the skills of data analysis. In these ways, the discourse of market and corporeal discipline converge in the neoliberal perspective, and the student and teacher must be forced to accept the right knowledge. The positivism of the neoliberal reforms tends to depoliticize knowledge while fostering conservative curricular content and pedagogical approaches on history, language arts, science, and mathematics. The neoconservative promotion of a cultural common core curriculum works symbiotically with the neoliberal tendency to promote knowledge that can be numerically quantified.

The trend to neoliberal educational models in the United States, though, cannot be separated from the events of 9/11 and the ensuing war on terror. 9/11 brought a heightened discourse on terrorism that framed the world in terms of civilization versus barbarism and claimed that all conflict required force, not diplomacy, for resolution. The discourse on terrorism allows powerful states to replace disputed values and ideologies with a focus on the method of fighting. The enemy can be interchangeable. The denial of politics at the core of the discourse on terrorism is a central part of the post-politics of neoliberal ideology and corresponds to the post-politics of neoliberal education. As the discourse of terrorism demands military enforcement of the neoliberal economic order public funds are captured for a series of imperial wars. At the same time, public education is defunded and aggressively privatized, and subject to capture by moneyed interests.

Since the launch of the war on terrorism and military assaults in Afghanistan, Iraq, Pakistan, and Yemen post 9/11 the United States has significantly increased its global military presence. Meanwhile it has simultaneously heightened the militarization of public education and vastly expanded the cultural pedagogies of militarism throughout civil society. While these moves might seem disconnected, it is our claim that any attention to the intersections between neoliberalism, education, and terrorism requires recognizing the ways that these shifts are interconnected and interdependent. Examples of the militarization of public education can be found in the expansion of the Troops to Teachers program, charter schools being opened as military academies, and the expansion of JROTC and ROTC programs, as well as the punitive and repressive militarized atmosphere that can be found especially in the schools of working class and poor students of color. The values of militarization—including a celebration of hierarchy, submission to authority, docility, and discipline—are shared by neoliberal educational models such as the Knowledge is Power Program (KIPP) and Edison Learning, which emphasize rigidity and conservative approaches to pedagogy such as scripted lessons and colonial forms of instruction particularly targeting working-class and poor students of color.[20]

As neoliberalism has promoted the investment in the repressive roles of the state and the gutting of its caregiving roles such as education, social spending has been redistributed to for-profit military industries. The vast spending on war fighting and the maintenance of a planet ringed by permanent military installments comes at the cost of the defunding of public schooling and other crucial public goods and services.

In 1983 the National Commission on Excellence in Education, directed by Reagan's Secretary of Education, released the *A Nation at Risk* report, which stated, "If an unfriendly foreign power had attempted to impose on America the mediocre educational performance that exists today, we might well have viewed it as an act of war."[21] The report was from an administration that had vowed to dismantle the Department of Education. It was significant, however, for framing the problems facing education as national security and global economic competition issues and setting the stage for educational reforms organized by these framing concerns. Likewise the Obama White House's recent *United States National Security Strategy* of 2010 frames education as primarily a matter of global economic competition in the "knowledge economy" (especially for science and engineering) and positions such competition as a matter of national security.[22] What these documents frame out are the crucial democratic roles that schools have in preparing critically minded citizens capable of collective self-governance. Such documents eschew the possibilities of students gaining insights from traditions in the humanities and social sciences to engage public problems such as struggles over public resources, environmental devastation, and the work of reconstructing the society in more just and egalitarian ways. As critical and public forms of teaching and learning are replaced by enforcement of knowledge, dissent, dialogue, and debate, the very lifeblood of democracy, become major casualties of the denial of politics found in neoliberalism, neoliberal education restructuring, and the discourse on terrorism.

The Geopolitics of Post-9/11 Higher Education Policy

> The war has unquestionably brought a new level of scrutiny to our politically correct campuses. Once the initial years of the campus culture war had passed, the public decided that campus leftism was either beyond the reach of anyone who hoped to do something about it, or irrelevant. The war changed that.
> —*Stanley Kurtz*[23]

On May 1, 2003, George W. Bush made a historic landing aboard the aircraft carrier USS *Lincoln* in order to formally announce the end of the war in Iraq.[24] Framed by a large banner announcing "Mission Accomplished," Bush congratulated U.S. troops, and reminded them that "in this battle, we have fought for the cause of liberty and for the peace of the world."[25] This event was a watershed moment for the war on terror. For supporters of the war, it served as a public display of victory and reinforced the notion of the United States as a benevolent superpower committed to "doing good" across the globe. For critics of the war, it stood as a paradigmatic example of how the U.S. government had managed to merge public concern over terrorism with government interest in controlling Iraq. It also served as a stunning illustration of how the rhetoric of American values had been used, yet again, to violate those values. The hubris and flamboyance of this moment attracted much attention from both supporters and critics of the war on terror—so much so that few noticed another presidential proclamation made that same day and few thought to reflect on the choice of May 1, May Day or the International Workers Day, for Bush's historic announcement of the end of the war.

Earlier on May 1, 2003, Bush issued a proclamation in honor of Loyalty Day, a legal U.S. holiday that has been officially observed since 1958.[26] In an effort to draw attention away from the communist- and socialist-inspired celebration of workers' rights associated with May Day, Loyalty Day was established as a day set aside "for the reaffirmation of loyalty to the United States and for the recognition of the heritage of American freedom."[27] Each president since 1958 has unsurprisingly used his proclamation to further his particular political agenda, and Bush's May 1, 2003, statement was no exception. What is of note, though, is the way that the 2003 proclamation emphasized the crucial role played by education in preparing students to sacrifice their lives to protect American values as they have been defined since 9/11. This goal is especially visible in the following quote:

> Our children need to know that our Nation is a force for good in the world, extending hope and freedom to others. By learning about America's history, achievements, ideas, and heroes, our young citizens will come to understand even more why freedom is worth protecting. Last September, I announced several initiatives that will help improve students' knowledge of American history, increase their civic involvement, and deepen their love for our great country.[28]

The speech that Bush gave in honor of those initiatives is worth reviewing because it sets the stage for the conflation of his two May 1, 2003, statements. On September 17, 2002, a little over a year after the attacks on the Twin Towers and the Pentagon, Bush highlighted his commitment to changing the way that children in the United States are taught:

> During the last year, our children have seen that lasting achievement in life comes through sacrifice and service. They've seen that evil is real, but that courage and justice can triumph. They've seen that America is a force for good in the world, bringing hope and freedom to other people. In recent events, our children have witnessed the great character of America. Yet they also need to know the great cause of America. They are seeing Americans fight for our country; they also must know why their country is worth fighting for.[29]

According to Bush, in order for future "missions" like that in Iraq to be "accomplished," the U.S. education system needs to collaborate by preparing students to have the proper view of the world and their place in it—a view that, by definition, would support the war on terror.

By considering Bush's "Mission Accomplished" speech and his Loyalty Day proclamation together, a number of key issues facing U.S. higher education post 9/11 are put into relief. Not only did the war on terror drastically change the relationship between the Unites States and the globe, often exacerbating trends we had already come to analyze, but the right-wing attacks on U.S. intellectuals and on higher education post 9/11 further revealed the combined effects of neoliberal policy and what might best be called *terror-think*. Terror-think after 9/11 was the culture of fear that followed the attacks and that created a sense of the United States as a country under constant threat. With regard to education, the threat was internal. Any professors who asked students to think critically about the United States were advancing the cause of the terrorists. The assaults on higher education since 9/11 have come from a variety of fronts, but they have all coalesced in a shared conviction that there is one true story to tell about America and it is one that supports the neoliberal, conservative, and fundamentalist project that dominated mainstream U.S. consciousness in the wake of the terrorist attacks.[30]

Considering Bush's two May Day activities in tandem underscores the fact that the post-9/11 assaults on higher education have benefited from the state of fear generated by the war on terror. As Stanley Kurtz makes clear in the opening epigraph to this section, the war on terror created an atmosphere conducive to scrutinizing higher education's role in matters of national security. The war requires loyalty and renewed patriotic vigor, which logically focused attention on the nation's youth and on those who educate them. Although it may be pure coincidence that these two presidential statements were uttered on the same historic day, their synchronicity demonstrates the degree to which the war on terror and the war on progressive, critical, left-oriented university teaching have been integrally related and complementary. For the U.S. public, and especially the nation's youth, to be sufficiently loyal to the war effort, it was essential that they unthinkingly accept statements like "Mission Accomplished." As Hugh Gusterson explains, "It is no coincidence that the right targeted dissent on campus after September 11."[31] The skilled minds that develop advanced weapon systems, economic models, and military strategies and speak the languages and understand the international cultures essential to the war on terror and to neoliberal globalization typically have been or will be trained in U.S. universities. Add to that the existence of "tenured radicals" and left-leaning, multicultural, postmodern curricula, which all threaten blind loyalty to the master narrative of *Pax Americana*, and it becomes clear why groups like The American Council of Trustees and Alumni (ACTA) characterized the university after 9/11 as the "weak link" in the war on terror.[32]

This section will focus on how post-9/11 education policy merged war on terror and neoliberal ideologies specifically with regard to programs related to teaching students about the United States and training them in international studies. In order to fully appreciate these connections, though, it is essential to recognize that post-9/11 higher education politics are a direct outgrowth of the right-wing rhetoric deployed during the McCarthy era and the culture wars. The tactics in use since 9/11 combine the politics of panic of the McCarthy era with fears that multiculturalism would lead to a devastating erosion of American national identity and values. Critics of the post-9/11 right-wing assault on higher education have tended to draw analogies to either the cold war or to the culture wars, but the post-9/11 efforts to discredit and defund higher education derive their tactics and ideological scaffolding from both periods.

One of the key ways to appreciate this trajectory is to note that these initiatives have been geopolitical. Post-9/11 right-wing education policy advocates a particular vision of the United States and the globe, one that is a direct outgrowth of American exceptionalism, *Pax Americana*, manifest destiny, the cold war, and neoliberal globalization. The geopolitical nature of these positions has led, consequently, to a focus on both the teaching of America and also of the globe. Regarding the teaching of the United States, we have critics like Lynne Cheney, cofounder of ACTA, who stressed that students need to learn more about the great character of America and who worried that too much attention was being paid to other cultures, or rather that other cultures were celebrated while the United States was criticized. In 1995, she wrote,

"As American students learn more about the faults of this country and the virtues of other nations, they will be less and less likely to think the country deserves their special support. They will not respond to calls to use American force...."[33] (quoted in Giroux and Searls Giroux 2004, 29). As Susan Searls Giroux points out, Cheney blamed multicultural educators for the "ideological disuniting of the nation," a practice that could produce "an increased unwillingness to wage all-out war."[34] On the global side, groups like Campus Watch have been dedicated to rectifying alleged bias in the teaching of the Middle East. They claim that "many U.S. scholars of the Middle East lack any appreciation of their country's national interests and often use their positions of authority to disparage these interests."[35] In short, they suggest that Middle East Studies professors are too sympathetic to the cultures they teach. Groups like Campus Watch have turned attention to the supposed anti-Americanism of area studies programs. Many critics of these threats to academic freedom have focused either on the assaults on American studies or on area studies, but these assaults are interrelated and must be considered as complementary. The post-9/11 attacks on higher education involve a two-pronged geopolitics that aims to alter the way that students understand the United States and also the world at large. Their shared agenda aims at policing both the study of "America" (understood narrowly) and the world so that the United States's global imperial project receives public support.

From the National Defense Education Act to the Defunding of Area Studies

> An educational emergency exists and requires action by the federal government. Assistance will come from Washington to help develop as rapidly as possible those skills essential to the national security.
> —*National Defense Education Act, 1958*[36]

On December 2, 1954, the Senate voted 67–22 to condemn Senator Joseph McCarthy, thereby ending the most sensational chapter of cold war interference in higher education. The next phase came only a few short months after McCarthy died on May 2, 1957, when the Soviet Union successfully launched Sputnik I, the world's first artificial satellite on October 4, 1957. The scientific supremacy of the Soviet Union sent a shock throughout the United States that led to a sense of educational inferiority. Shortly afterward, in 1958, Congress passed the National Defense Education Act (NDEA), legislation appropriating funds for student college loans and for curriculum development in science, math, and foreign languages. Prior to the NDEA there had been strong opposition to any federal involvement in higher education, but Sputnik I had launched a national emergency. After 9/11, in congressional debates over a new version of the NDEA, now called the College Access and Opportunity Act, which covers Title VI appropriations for area studies, Republican politicians attempted to generate a similar atmosphere of fear in order to justify an increased supervisory role for the federal government. The post-9/11 legislation, like that of the original NDEA that spawned it, promotes a specific worldview, where the vision of the United States as the exceptional and unique center of the globe depends on American and area studies for its ideological support.

Although there is much debate about the origins of both area studies and American studies, the general consensus is that the cold war played a defining role in shaping each of these fields by establishing the "state/intelligence/foundation" nexus that supplied the funding and, consequently, influenced the intellectual agenda.[37] For instance at the federal level, Title VI of the NDEA was dedicated to fostering foreign language study for use in national defense and was responsible for the growth of area studies programs. In another key example, the Congress for Cultural Freedom run by the CIA from 1950 to 1967 promoted the "American way" and supported an international propaganda machine that endeavored to convince Western European intellectuals that communism was antithetical to creativity.[38] In addition, organizations like the Carnegie Corporation, the Rockefeller Foundation, and the Ford Foundation pumped millions of dollars into American and area studies.[39]

As Doug Henwood explains, the geopolitics of the cold war required the collaboration of American studies and area studies in the construction of a worldview "that allowed us to understand our unique fitness for our postwar role as the world's governor, and encouraged a finer appreciation of our cultural sophistication among the ruled."[40] This view would change as a result of the radical politics of the 1960s. Assumptions of cultural superiority and exceptionalism were replaced by theories of economic dependence and cultural imperialism. Eurocentrism unraveled in favor of identity politics. Masao Miyoshi notes that the worldwide student revolts of the 1960s shared a number of common beliefs that forever changed U.S. academic life. These rebellions gave voice to "an intense revulsion for cold war repression both in the East and the West" as well as to a "newly aroused skepticism about dominant central power."[41] These revolutions eventually led to fundamental ideological shifts in area and American studies that aimed, first, to reassess these fields' complicity with dominant power and, second, to redirect that power to the disenfranchised. In the aftermath of the 1960s, during the culture wars, academics called for post-area studies and post-national American studies in efforts to distance their work from the perceived ideological bias of their predecessors.

During the culture wars faculty in both fields came under attack from the right for destroying the foundations of western civilization. If the world could no longer be divided into superior and inferior cultures, and, if there were no absolute cultural values, then how to explain the dominance of certain nations, like the United States, over others? Even though such critical shifts served to shake the foundations of U.S. exceptionalism, these changes did not arouse the level of panic encountered by American and area studies post 9/11. This distinction is explained, in part, by the right's ambivalence regarding globalization. As Miyoshi notes, "by the end of the Cold War, around 1990, the hegemony of the state was replaced by the dominant power of the global market."[42] For globalization to be successful consumers needed to have a less provincial worldview, one which, for instance, would allow them to purchase products made in other nations. Thus the post-nationalism of American and area studies intersected with the rise of global capitalism.[43] Funding for American and area studies underwent a transition in the post-Nixon years that increasingly urged these fields to embrace a global perspective. Global capitalism replaced national security as the prime ideological motor for state and foundation sponsorship of these fields. For example, congressional re-appropriation of Title VI area studies funds since the 1980s has stressed outreach programs that would "educate" the citizenry about foreign cultures. Such programs ostensibly prepare the public to appreciate a world governed by global trade agreements rather than by cold war regional divisions.

After 9/11, ambivalence over the global views of American and area studies underwent a dramatic shift. While globalization required a more multicultural view of the world so that U.S. citizens would be more comfortable with the power of multinational corporations, the war on terror could not afford such cultural relativity. It is important to note that the attention to world cultures and the commitment to international literacy found in many contemporary university curricula appealed to both international business and to progressive leftists critical of U.S. hegemony. The problem for the right-wing culture warriors was that they perceived that the bulk of these courses and the faculty that taught them undermined the goals of international business and threatened U.S. capitalist interests. Yet, they had a difficult time articulating their agenda because they still wanted courses on global culture, but they wanted only those that supported U.S. neoliberalism. This problem was quickly resolved when the 9/11 attacks facilitated the linkage of globalization with nationalism. The extreme patriotism of the White House coupled with imperial designs on world oil led to a renewed interest in reviving global divisions similar to those of the cold war. Since 9/11 the conservative, right-wing assault on higher education has capitalized on the emergency state caused by the war on terror in order to accuse American and area studies of insufficient national loyalty and outright support of terrorism.

Area and international studies faculty, courses, and programs were accused after 9/11 of profound anti-Americanism. Scholars of the Middle East, most notably Edward Said and those who align themselves with his work, came under harsh attack and were accused of being terrorist infiltrators hell-bent on brainwashing the nation's students and undermining U.S. national security. Because the United States has been painted as a nation under siege since 9/11, the Right has argued that academia has to commit to the war effort. This means allowing military recruiters access to students, training students to serve the nation, and teaching a curriculum that supports the war on terror. American studies, accordingly, is expected to teach the greatness of the nation passively, uncritically, and undemocratically. Ironically, though, such a curriculum poses a problem for area studies. Paul Bové argues that there is an inherent contradiction between the dominant ideological programs of American and area studies. On the one hand, American studies should not produce any new knowledge about America nor should it "produce knowledge essential to the decision making of state policy."[44] American studies remains important to the state merely as a tool for internal propaganda and for export: it "allows the state to deploy the symbolic values and signifying practices of various cultural elements within the nation."[45] On the other hand, area studies "was created to meet a policy need to allow greater success in its own expansion and development."[46] Hence, scholars and students of area studies must first believe in the mission of the United States, passively and uncritically, only to then commit to actively—but also uncritically—producing new knowledge about the globe that can serve U.S. interests. It stands to reason, then, that the war on terror has required renewed government oversight of both American and area studies.

This is the context within which Congress proposed the most invasive higher education legislation in U.S. history. Title VI funds dedicated to supporting area and language studies underwent reauthorization as part of the International Studies in Higher Education Act of 2003 or HR 3077. The bill passed the House, but never reached a Senate vote. A new version was under consideration as HR 509, the International Studies in Higher Education Act of 2005, and also as HR 609, the College Access and Opportunity Act of 2005, but this also never became law. Even though these versions of the law did not pass, the debates over them reveal much about the political lobbying regarding the teaching of global studies since 9/11. In the opening statement introducing the legislation, Subcommittee Chairman Patrick Tiberi clearly linked the bill with both the war on terror and a neoliberal political agenda: "Today's integrated world and global marketplace underscores the importance of training these specialists who can provide assistance to the government and the private sector, and communicate across cultures on our behalf. In addition, we are more aware than ever that America's security needs require advanced international knowledge and effective foreign language skills."[47] The opening language of the bill echoes right-wing rhetoric like that of Lynne Cheney and President Bush, who suggest that international studies must serve national interests and ultimately prepare the nation's youth to sacrifice themselves for homeland security: "The events and aftermath of September 11, 2001, have underscored the need for the nation to strengthen and enhance American knowledge of international relations, world regions, and foreign languages. Homeland security and effective United States engagement abroad depend upon an increased number of Americans who have received such training and are willing to serve their nation."[48] Students need to be willing to defend their nation's international interests, and such training requires the collaboration of American and area studies in advancing a worldview where the United States is the global center of all that is good.

The most substantial and disturbing change to Title VI government funding for area studies in the 2005 version of the bill was the creation of an International Advisory Board whose mission was "to improve the programs under this title to better reflect the national needs related to the homeland security, international education, and international affairs."[49] In hearings before the House on June 19, 2003, Kurtz, one of the most vociferous advocates of the advisory board, argued that the federal government needed to radically reassess the nature of funding for international study. According to Kurtz:

> The ruling intellectual paradigm in academic area studies (especially Middle Eastern Studies) is called "post-colonial theory." . . . The core premise of post-colonial theory is that it is immoral for a scholar to put his knowledge of foreign languages and cultures at the service of American power.[50]

Despite the fact that Kurtz's assessment of the "core premise" of postcolonial theory is patently false and totally unsubstantiated, it remained the case that throughout these debates post-colonial theory was targeted as a critical practice at the service of terrorism.

Even though the version of the bill with the advisory board never passed, it is worth noting that the idea of the advisory board indicated new degrees of federal intervention in higher education that far exceeded that of the cold war. The broad authority given to this board conflicted with the earlier provisions of the NDEA that expressly prohibited direct interference in academic matters: "Nothing in this act shall be construed to authorize any agency or employee of the United States to exercise any direction, supervision, or control over the curriculum, program of instruction, administration, or personnel of any educational institution or school system."[51] Of course, such language rings false after the multiple exposed scandals that linked the government and intelligence community to faculty and specific academic projects. Nevertheless, the revised 2005 version of the NDEA takes government oversight a step further. That version of the bill reads:

> Nothing in this title shall be construed to authorize the International Advisory Board to mandate, direct, or control an institution of higher education's specific instructional content, curriculum, or program of instruction. The Board is authorized to study, monitor, apprise, and evaluate a sample of activities supported under this title in order to provide recommendations to the Secretary and the Congress for the improvement of programs under the title and to ensure programs meet the purposes of the title.[52]

In contrast with the cold war legislation, the advisory board would have had the ability to monitor syllabi and curricula, even though they technically could not control them. It is also interesting to note that the board's limitations no longer included supervision of faculty or administrators, whereas the 1958 version specifically prohibited government interference in personnel and administration.

Without question the purpose of the board was to exercise greater ideological control over university programs that received federal grant money. The post-9/11 environment was conducive to a culture of suspicion that facilitated arguments that faculty might be brainwashing students, supporting terrorists, and bashing the United States. Response to the creation of the advisory board for Title VI grants was strong, and it was eventually dropped from the version of the Higher Education Act that finally passed in 2008, five years late and after an unprecedented 14 extensions of the statutory deadline. The delay in passing this legislation reveals the extent to which federal support of higher education had become intensely politicized after 9/11. In the version of the bill that did become law one key ideological component was preserved: "Applications for funding must explain how the funded activities will reflect diverse perspectives and a wide range of views and generate debate on world regions and international affairs. Applications must also describe how the applicant will encourage government service in areas of national need."[53] This language reflected the ongoing right-wing assertion that students were not presented with diverse views in their classes—phrasing that was code for saying that right-wing views were excluded. There isn't sufficient space here to parse this debate and to show how the argument has shifted since the era of the culture wars, but the consequence of including this language was that it opened up the possibility for conservative groups to claim that they were supporting diversity by advocating for the increased inclusion of their views in the classroom.

The versions of the Higher Education Act that circulated after 9/11 not only exposed the way that terror was recruited as an ideological weapon that helped create an atmosphere of suspicion on college campuses, but also revealed the ways that neoliberalism and terror interconnected to radically alter how universities receive state and federal support. Almost uniformly the economic crisis was used to justify massive cuts at the state level: the dissolution of academic unions and the elimination of entire programs, almost all of which were in the humanities—the fields most often linked to left-leaning academics.

Of interest, though, is the fact that after 9/11 greater federal support existed for international education initiatives via programs like Title VI and the Fulbright Scholar Program. While ideological debates about patriotism circulated in the immediate aftermath of 9/11, this was one area of humanities-oriented higher education that saw an increase in federal funds. This would all change under the Obama administration when neoliberal academic agendas would come into full force through the work of Arne Duncan, Obama's Secretary of Education. As Henry Giroux explains, "In Arne Duncan's world, the language of educational reform is defined primarily through the modalities of competition, measurement, and quantification."[54] Critical thinking, global awareness, and engaged citizenship are displaced as goals for education by test scores, outcomes, and patriotism. In the center of these shifts are massive adjustments in federal and state support for higher education as universities depend more and more on corporate dollars. Thus, in the most recent attacks on Title VI International Education and Foreign Language programs, the Department of Education sidestepped the ideological debates that had been the hallmark of the Bush era. Instead under Obama and Duncan funds simply disappeared with no other explanation than the economic crisis. The 2011 cuts to federal funding for higher education are the most extensive in decades.[55] Title VI programs saw a decrease in total funding from $125.9 million in FY 2010 to $75.7 million in FY 2011, a reduction of approximately 40 percent. Title VI Domestic Programs would receive $66.7 million in FY 2011 as opposed to $108.4 million in FY 2010. The Fulbright-Hays program (grants for doctoral research abroad) was cut from $15.6 million in FY 2010 to $7.5 million in FY 2011. The Institute for International Public Policy dropped to $1.6 million from $1.9 million in FY 2010. In addition, the Javits Fellowship program that awards graduate students in the social sciences, humanities, and arts saw its funding of $9.7 million reduced by $1.6 million, or 16.5 percent. The Department simply eliminated the Thurgood Marshall Legal Scholarships, a $3 million program to help underrepresented minorities prepare for law school. As the Consortium of Social Science Associations notes, "Other programs eliminated are some of the small programs that previous administrations have sought unsuccessfully to end many times. These include: Women's Educational Equity ($2.4 million); Close-Up Fellowships ($.19 million); Academies for American History and Civics ($1.8 million); Javits Gifted and Talented ($7.5 million); and Civic Education-We the People ($21.6 million), the rest of Civic Education was reduced by $12.2 million or over 91 percent."[56] In contrast, the Obama administration increased Race to the Top funding by $699 million, adding a new provision allowing states to use the funds for early childhood education grants. Henry Giroux and Kenneth Saltman have called Race to the Top funding "the market-based and penal model of pedagogy." These cuts indicate how the culture of fear linked with market-driven practices to defund federal support for education in ways unimaginable prior to 9/11.

Conclusion: Despair or Hope?

With all due respect to Charles Dickens, it now appears to be the *worst* of times for education in America; but at the same time, amid all of the despair and foolishness on the part of right-wing politicians and conservative and corporate interests, it is not entirely clear that the spring of hope is beyond reach. At the moment, workers and young people are marching and demonstrating all over the globe against the dictates, values, and policies of a market-driven economy that has corrupted politics, pushed democracy to its vanishing point, and undermined public values. Higher education, along with a number of other public spheres necessary to keep civic values alive, is being challenged in a way that both baffles and shocks anyone who believes in the ideals and promises of a substantive democracy. In the United States, union-busting politicians such as governors Scott Walker of Wisconsin and Chris Christie of New Jersey not only want to gut social services and sell them off to the highest bidder, but also are symptomatic of a political fringe movement that wants to destroy the critical formative cultures, dedicated public servants, and institutions that give any sense of vitality, substance, and hope to higher education in the United States. As the meaning of democracy is betrayed by its transformation into a market society, corporate power and money appear unchecked in their ability to privatize, deregulate, and destroy all vestiges of public life. In a post-

9/11 world, neoliberalism has proven to be a death sentence on democracy.

America's military wars abroad are now matched by the war at home; that is, the wars in Iraq and Afghanistan have found their counterpart in the war against the poor, immigrants, young people, students, unions, public sector workers, the welfare state, and educators. The call for shared sacrifices on the part of conservatives and Tea Party extremists becomes code for destroying the social state, preserving and increasing the power of megarich corporations, and securing the wealth of the top one percent of the population with massive tax breaks while placing the burden of the current global economic meltdown on the shoulders of students, young people, African Americans, low-skilled workers, and the poor. Deficit reductions and austerity policies that allegedly address the global economic meltdown caused by the financial hawks running Wall Street now do the real work of stripping teachers of their collective bargaining rights, dismantling programs long associated with social services, and relegating young people to mind-deadening curricula and a debt-ridden future. As training replaces critical education, higher education is increasingly shaped in the interests of market values, social practices, and modes of governance. Faculty become entrepreneurs, students are relegated to customers, and knowledge is sold to the highest bidder. The notion of higher education as a democratic public sphere recedes from public memory just as it is under attack as in no other time in American history.

Feelings of despair and disposability, as well as unnecessary human suffering, now engulf large swaths of the American people, often pushing them into situations that are not merely tragic but life threatening. A survival of the fittest ethic has replaced any reasonable notion of solidarity, social responsibility, and compassion for the other. Ideology does not seem to matter any longer as right-wing Republicans have less interest in argument and persuasion than in bullying their alleged enemies with the use of heavy-handed legislation and necessary dire threats, as when Wisconsin's Republican Governor Walker threatened to mobilize the National Guard to prevent teachers' unions from protesting their possible loss of bargaining rights and a host of anti-worker proposals.

With any viable leadership lacking at the national level, young people and workers are both watching the movements for democracy that are taking place all over the globe, but especially in the volatile Arab nations and Western Europe. Struggles abroad give Americans a glimpse of what happens when individual solutions to collective problems lose their legitimacy as a central tenet of neoliberal ideology. Massive demonstrations, pitched street battles, nonviolent gatherings, the impressive use of the new media as an alternative political and educational tool, and an outburst of long-repressed anger eager for collective action are engulfing many countries across the globe. In smaller numbers, such protests are also taking place in a number of cities around the United States. Many Americans are once again invoking democracy, rejecting its association with empty formalities and as a legitimating discourse to justify political systems that produce massive forms of wealth and income inequality. Democracy's promises are laying bare the sordid realities that now speak in its name. Its energy is becoming infectious, and one can only hope that those who believe that education is the foundation of critical agency, politics, and democracy itself will be drawn to the task of fighting America's move in the past thirty years to a politically and economically authoritarian system. At stake here is the need for a new vocabulary, vision, and politics that will unleash a new democratic vision capable of imagining a life and society free of the dictates of endless military wars, boundless material waste, extreme inequality, disposable populations, and unfounded human suffering. Higher education now more than ever must be viewed as central to any viable notion of politics. If real reform is going to happen, a sustainable, critical, formative culture has to be put in place that supports notions of engaged citizenship, civic courage, public values, democratic modes of governing, and a genuine belief in freedom, equality, and justice. And this is precisely what higher education should do. Ideas matter as do the human beings and institutions that make them count—including those intellectuals both in and out of schools who bear the responsibility to provide the conditions for the American public of all ages to be able to think critically so they can act imaginatively, so they can embrace a vision of the good life as a just life, one that extends the values, practices, and visions of democracy to everyone.

1

Militarizing Higher Education, Neoliberalism's Culture of Depravity, and Democracy's Demise after 9/11

Henry A. Giroux

> Lacking the truth, [we] will however find *instants of truth*, and those instants are in fact all we have available to us to give some order to this chaos of horror. These instants arise spontaneously, like oases in the desert. They are anecdotes and they reveal in their brevity what it is all about.... This is what happens when men decide to turn the world upside down.
> —Hannah Arendt[1]

Militarized Knowledge and Monstrous Subjectivities

Since the tragic events of 9/11, state-sanctioned violence, and the formative culture that makes it possible, have increasingly made their way into higher education. Although there is a long history of higher education taking on research funds and projects that serve the military–industrial complex, such projects were often hidden from public view. When they did become public, they provoked student protests and opposition, especially during the 1960s. What is new today is that more research projects in higher education than ever before are being funded by various branches of the military, but either no one is paying attention or no one seems to care. Ethical and political considerations about the role of the university in a democratic society have given way to a hyper-pragmatism couched in the language of austerity and political orthodoxy, largely driven by a decrease in state funding for higher education and the dire lack of jobs for many graduates. It is also driven by a market-centered ethos that celebrates a militant form of individualism, a survivalist ethic, a crass emphasis on materialism, a notion of public space overrun by privatized concerns, and an utter disregard of responsibility for others.[2] Similarly, as research funds dry up for programs aimed at addressing crucial social problems, new opportunities open up with the glut of military funding aimed at creating more sophisticated weapons, surveillance technologies, and modes of armed knowledge that connect anthropological concerns with winning wars.[3]

Higher education should be one place where young people learn to question the framing mechanisms that allow them both to be turned into producers and consumers of violence and to become increasingly indifferent to matters of social and moral responsibility. Military modes of education, largely driven by the demands of war and organized violence, are investing heavily in pedagogical practices that train students in various intelligence operations. Programs such as the Pat Roberts Intelligence Scholars Program and the Intelligence Community Scholarship Program disregard the principles of academic freedom and recruit students to serve in a number of intelligence agencies, such as the CIA, which have a long history of using torture, assassinations, and illegal prisons, and on occasion committing domestic atrocities—extending from the FBI's intelligence and counterinsurgency operation called COINTELPRO, which illegally targeted progressives and antiwar activists during the 1950s, 1960s, and 1970s, to the more recent revelation regarding the Bush administration's spying on Juan Cole, a prominent academic and critic of the Iraq War.[4] The increasingly intensified and expansive symbiosis between the military–industrial complex and academia is also on full display with the creation of the "Minerva Consortium," ironically named after the goddess of wisdom, whose purpose is to fund various universities to "carry out social sciences research relevant to national security."[5] As David Price has brilliantly documented, the CIA and other intelligence agencies

> today sneak unidentified students with undisclosed links to intelligence agencies into university classrooms. A new generation of so-called flagship programs have quietly taken root on campuses, and, with each new flagship, our universities are transformed into vessels of the militarized state.[6]

The Pentagon's desire to turn universities into militarized knowledge factories producing ideas, research, and personnel in the interest of the Homeland (In)Security State should be of special concern for intellectuals, artists, academics, and others who believe that the university should oppose such interests and alignments.[7] Connecting universities with any one of the 15 U.S. security and intelligence agencies replaces the ideal of educating students to be critical citizens with the notion of students as potential spies and citizen soldiers.[8] Pedagogy, in this instance, becomes militarized.

Militarization suggests more than simply a militaristic ideal—with its celebration of war as the truest measure of the health of the nation and the soldier-warrior as the most noble expression of the merging of masculinity and unquestioning patriotism. It suggests an intensification and expansion of the underlying values, practices, ideologies, social relations, and cultural representations associated with military culture. The values of militarization are no longer restricted to foreign-policy ventures; the ideals of war in a post-9/11 world have become normalized, serving as a powerful educational force that shapes our lives, memories, and daily experiences.

The military has become a way of life, producing modes of education, goods, jobs, communication, and institutions that exceed traditional understandings of the role, territory, and place of the military in American society. Military values, social relations, and practices now bleed into every aspect of American life. What is distinctive about the militarization of the social order is that war becomes a source of pride rather than alarm, while organized violence is elevated to a place of national honor, recycled endlessly through a screen culture that bathes in blood, death, and war porn. As democratic idealism is replaced by the combined forces of the military–industrial complex, civil liberties are gradually eroded along with the formative culture in which the dictates of militarization can be challenged. Wars abroad also further accentuate the failure to address serious problems at home. As Andrew Bacevich points out, "Fixing Iraq or Afghanistan ends up taking precedent over fixing Cleveland and Detroit."[9] Cities rot; unemployment spreads; bridges collapse; veterans are refused adequate medical care; youth lack jobs and hope—and yet the permanent warfare state squanders more than a trillion dollars waging wars in Iraq and Afghanistan. As Kevin Baker points out, "We now substitute military solutions for almost everything, including international alliances, diplomacy, effective intelligence agencies, democratic institutions—even national security. . . . The logic is inexorable."[10] A primitive tribalism now grips society as our democratic institutions and public spheres become inseparable from the military. Even as the wars in Iraq and Afghanistan wind down, the U.S. military budget continues to grow. While global military expenditures total over $7.1 trillion, "The USA is responsible for 41 percent of the world total, distantly followed by China (8.2 percent of world share), Russia (4.1 percent), UK and France (both 3.6 percent)."[11]

As higher education is weakened through an ongoing assault by right-wing ideologues, corporate power, and the forces of militarization, the very idea of the university as a site of critical thinking, public service, and socially responsible research is in danger of disappearing. This is especially true as the national security state, the Pentagon, and corporate power set their sights on restructuring higher education at a time when it is vulnerable because of a loss of revenue and a growing public disdain toward critical thinking, faculty autonomy, and the public mission of the university. Higher education has been targeted because when it aligns its modes of governance, knowledge production, and view of learning with the forces of neoliberal capitalism and the mechanisms of violence and disposability, it makes a belief in commodified and militarized knowledge a part of everyday life. Imposing new forms of discipline, affective investments, modes of knowledge, and values conducive to a public willing to substitute training for education, a corporatized and militarized mode of pedagogy removes ethical considerations from the social and human costs produced by the market and the permanent warfare state. More specifically, higher education in this instance makes possible a belief in militarized and instrumental knowledge as a fact of life while legitimating those social processes "in which civil society organizes itself for the production of violence."[12]

More is at stake here than the corruption of academic fields, faculties, and the overall ideal of the university as a democratic public sphere. There is the total transformation of the state from a liberal social state into a punishing state. The machinery of death is more than a technology; it is also driven by a formative culture that creates the knowledge, values, and practices that enable human beings to work in the service of violence and death. When the military increasingly becomes a model for shaping the most basic institutions of society—institutions ranging from public schools and industry to higher education—the ideals of democracy become a faint memory and American society plunges into barbarism on all fronts. The militarization and neoliberalization of higher education are thus inextricably linked to the intensification of a general moral coma that now hangs over American society, representing one of the most disturbing legacies of the war on terror. The war on terror that began with the tragic events of 9/11 has not only produced a culture of insecurity and fear in which critical inquiry and dissent are frowned upon, it has also combined with neoliberalism's disdain for the social state to produce modes of subjectivities that can at best be called monstrous.

Marked by a virulent notion of hardness and aggressive masculinity, a culture and public pedagogy of depravity have become commonplace in a society in which pain, humiliation, and abuse are condensed into digestible spectacles of violence endlessly circulated through extreme sports, reality TV, video games, YouTube postings, and proliferating forms of the new and old media. But the ideology of hardness and the economy of pleasure it justifies are also present in the material relations of power that have reigned virtually unchecked since the Reagan presidency, when a shift in government policies first took place and set the stage for the emergence of torture and state violence under the Bush-Cheney regime. This shift moved the state further away from providing social protections and safeguarding civil liberties toward the unleashing of precarious market forces alongside the establishment of legislative programs intent on promoting shared fears and increasing disciplinary modes of governance that criminalize social problems and inflict forms of punishment on the disadvantaged.[13] Today, conservative and liberal politicians alike are willing to spend millions waging wars around the globe, funding the largest military state in the world, providing huge tax benefits to the ultra-rich and major corporations, and all the while draining public coffers, increasing the scale of human poverty and misery, and eliminating all viable public spheres—whether they be the social state, public schools, public transportation, or any other aspect of a culture that addresses the needs of the common good.

Meanwhile, as suggested above, exaggerated violence now rules not only screen culture but the discourse of government officials. The public pedagogy of entertainment includes extreme images of violence, human suffering, and torture splashed across giant movie screens, some in 3D, offering viewers every imaginable portrayal of violent acts, each more shocking and brutal than the last. What is appalling about this glut of screen violence and cruelty is that it becomes a resource for many politicians who mimic its values and legitimate its politics. For instance, the Republican party leadership in 2011, in an effort to rally its members in the budget battle with the Obama administration, played a short clip from the Ben Affleck movie *The Town*. The exchange between Affleck and one of friends played by Jeremy Renner goes as follows: Ben Affleck: "I need your help. I can't tell you what it is. You can never ask me about it later. And we're going to hurt some people." Jeremy Renner: "Whose car are we going to take?"[14] What Affleck and Renner then do is proceed to put on hockey masks, break into an apartment, bludgeon two men with sticks, and shoot another in the leg. Images of mind-crushing punishment and cruelty now provide the framework for establishing legislative practices among a group of right-wing extremists who are shaping policy in the United States. This is not merely barbarism parading as theater for political reform—it is also a blatant indicator of the degree to which sadism and the infatuation with violence have become normalized in a society that seems to take delight in dehumanizing itself.

As the social is devalued along with reason, ethics, and any vestige of democracy, spectacles of violence and brutality now merge into forms of collective pleasure that constitute what I believe is an important and new symbiosis between visual pleasure, violence, and suffering. Revelling in the suffering of others should never be reduced merely to a matter of individual pathology, but more today than ever before it is possible to detect how taking unquestioned delight in others' pain registers a larger economy of pleasure across the broader culture and social landscape. My emphasis here is on the sadistic impulse and how it merges spectacles of violence and brutality with forms of collective pleasure. This is what I call the *depravity of aesthetics*—the emergence of a new aesthetic of amplified voyeurism characteristic of a social order that has narrowed the range of social expression and values, turning instead to the pursuit of pleasure and the receipt of instant gratification as its sole imperatives. Before building on the contemporary relationship between aesthetics and violence, I will draw upon prior discussions of the aestheticization of human suffering in order to underscore what has shifted in the educational function of the broader culture since the aesthetics of depravity was conceptualized, and what educational issues are at stake in the emerging depravity of aesthetics.

The Aesthetics of Depravity

Susan Sontag believed that capitalist societies require images in order to infiltrate the culture of everyday life, legitimate official power, and anaesthetize their subjects through visual spectacles.[15] Such images also enable the circulation of information along with militaristic modes of surveillance and control. Sontag argued in her later work that war and photography have become inseparable, and, as a result of that fusion, representations of violence no longer compelled occasions for self and social critique. Rather, shocking images increasingly emerged as a mode of entertainment, advancing the machinery of consumption and undermining democratic relations and social formations. She was particularly concerned about an aesthetics of depravity—that is, an aesthetics that traffics in images of human suffering that are subordinated to the formal properties of beauty, design, and taste—thus serving in the main to "bleach out a moral response to what is shown."[16] For Sontag and many other critical theorists, the aesthetics of depravity reveals itself when it takes as its transcendent object the misery of others—murderous displays of torture, mutilated bodies, and intense suffering—while simultaneously erasing the names, histories, and voices of the victims of such brutal and horrible

CHAPTER 1

acts. What is worth noting, especially in the current historical context, is that a perverse pleasure seems to be had in the erasure of the victims' names, voices, and histories. Paul Virilio, in a meditation on the extermination of bodies and the environment from Auschwitz to Chernobyl, refers to this depraved form of art as an "aesthetics of disappearance that would come to characterize the whole fin-de-siècle" of the twentieth century.[17] An example of this mode of aesthetics was on full display in the mainstream media's coverage of the photographs depicting the torture of prisoners at Abu Ghraib prison. As Mark Reinhardt points out, the dominant media had no qualms about showing the faces of the victims, thus violating their dignity, but expressed widespread indignation over reproducing the naked bodies of the victims, claiming that it would demonstrate bad taste.[18] In this instance, concerns of beauty and etiquette displaced subject matter, while sheltering the viewer from any sense of complicity in such crimes.

Needless to say, Abu Ghraib was not an isolated event; the desire to view such voluptuous depravity had been honed for decades. Since the early 1990s, Benetton, the famous clothing manufacturer, had shown that trafficking in pain and human suffering is not only good for business but also good for providing a patina of legitimacy to the company as an artsy brand with philanthropic concerns.[19] Benetton's United Colours campaign appropriated shocking and visually arresting representations of violence and pain in order to sell clothes and attract global attention to its brand. In doing so, Benetton did more than conjoin the worlds of beauty and suffering; it also pushed a mode of commercial advertising in which the subjects of often horrendous misfortunes and acts of suffering disappeared into the all-embracing world of logos and brand names. For example, Benetton used the colorized image of David Kirby, a dying AIDS patient, to sell jumpers. A more poignant example of the reconfiguring of the aesthetic in order to exploit images of suffering can be found in an unpublished interview in which Jacqueline

Lichtenstein recounts her experience visiting the museum at Auschwitz. She writes:

> When I visited the Museum at Auschwitz, I stood in front of the display cases. What I saw there were images from contemporary art and I found that absolutely terrifying. Looking at the exhibits of suitcases, prosthetics, children's toys, I didn't feel frightened. I didn't collapse. I wasn't completely overcome the way I had been walking around the camp. No. In the Museum, I suddenly had the impression I was in a museum of contemporary art. I took the train back, telling myself that they had won! They had won since they'd produced forms of perception that are all of a piece with a mode of destruction they made their own.[20]

As we move into the second decade of the twenty-first century, ethical considerations and social costs are further eclipsed by market-driven policies and values. Images of human suffering are increasingly abstracted from social and political contexts and the conditions that make such suffering possible—and thus made more visually alluring. Moreover, as public issues collapse into privatized considerations, matters of agency, responsibility, and ethics are now framed within the discourse of extreme individualism. According to this neoliberal logic, individuals and the problems they confront are removed from any larger consideration of public values, social responsibility, and compassion. The collapse of the social and the formative culture that makes human bonds possible is now outmatched, though hardly defeated, by the rise of a Darwinian ethic of greed and self-interest in which violence, aggressiveness, and sadism have become the primary metric for living and dying. As the social contract is replaced by social collapse, a culture of cruelty has emerged in American society. This new mode of collective behavior resembles Freud's theory of the death drive, although it is reconfigured less as a desire to return to nothingness (and thus quiet forever dangerous sensations) than as the apogee of an eternal present of titillation, achieved through the serial production, circulation, and consumption of images of death. Increasingly, as the spectacle of violence permeates every aspect of the machinery of cultural production and screen culture, desire seems only to come alive when people are aroused by spectacles of high-intensity violence and images of death, mutilation, and suffering.

Death and violence have become the mediating link between America's domestic policy—the state's treatment of its own citizens—and U.S. foreign policy, between the tedium of ever expanding workdays and the thrill of sadistic release. Disposable bodies now waste away in American prisons, schools, and shelters just as they litter the battlefields of Iraq and Afghanistan. America has become a permanent warfare state, with a deep investment in a cultural politics and the corollary cultural apparatuses to legitimate and sanctify its machinery of death. The American public's fascination with violence and death is obvious not only in the recent popular obsession with vampire and zombie films and books; we also see it in serious Hollywood films such as the 2010 Academy Award–winning *The Hurt Locker*, in which the American bomb disposal expert, William James (Jeremy Renner), repeatedly puts himself at risk in the face of defusing various bomb threats—thus to highlight the filmmaker's concern with a growing "addiction" to war. As Mark Featherstone points out, there is more represented here than the reckless behavior of immature and hyper-masculine soldiers. He writes that James

> takes unnecessary risks and lives for the limit experience. . . . [H]e feels most alive when he is closest to death, a condition supported by the philosopher Martin Heidegger, who spoke about being-towards-death, and told us that we should live every moment as though it was our last, in order that we might live a full and meaningful life. When James . . . throws the bomb suit away and stands before the bomb with no protection, he puts himself at the mercy of the bomb, the embodiment of the death drive. Herein lies James' ethic of deadly risk, his attempt to realize Heidegger's idea, being-

towards-death, in what for Freud would be a perverse form, being-with-bombs.... In Freudian/Kleinian terms, the bomb is also a projection of the self because it consists of a hard shell containing powerful explosive material.[21]

To be sure, Featherstone coarsens Heidegger's concept of "being-towards-death," but his notion of the "hard shell" echoes Theodor Adorno's reference to an ideology of hardness that Adorno believed was one of the root causes of the Holocaust.[22] According to Adorno, violence became entrenched in German culture as the rituals of aggression, brutality, and sadism became a bureaucratized and normalized part of everyday life. More specifically, Adorno believed the "inability to identify with others was unquestionably the most important psychological condition for the fact that something like Auschwitz could have occurred in the midst of more or less civilized and innocent people."[23] One of the consequences of this psychological state was the production of a virulent masculinity that augured both a pathological relationship with the body, pain, and violence, and a disdain for compassion, human rights, and social justice. More than a trace of this mode of aggression and moral indifference now dominates contemporary American society.

The broader cultural turn toward the death drive and the strange economy of desire it produces is also evident in the emergence of a culture of cruelty in which the American public appears more and more amenable to deriving pleasure from images that portray gratuitous violence and calamity. Such portrayals give credence to Walter Benjamin's claim that in late modernity the mesmerizing and seductive language of power underlies captivating spectacles that inextricably fuse aesthetics with fascist politics.[24] To his credit, Benjamin recognized the affective force of aesthetics and its, at times, perverse ability to "privilege cultural forms over ethical norms" while mobilizing emotions, desires, and pleasures that delight in human suffering and become parasitic upon the pain of others.[25] Benjamin's notion of the aesthetic and its relation to fascism is important, in spite of appearing deterministic, because it highlights how fascist spectacles use the force of titillating sensations and serve to privilege the emotive and visceral at the expense of thoughtful engagement. In his analysis of Benjamin's notion of the aesthetic, Lutz Koepnick develops this point further by exploring how the fascist aesthetic "mobilizes people's feelings primarily to neutralize their senses, massaging minds and emotions so that the individual succumbs to the charisma of vitalistic power."[26]

Rather than reject the aesthetics of depravity as being exclusively tied to the pleasure of consumption and the spectacle of violence, if not fascism itself, Sontag modified Benjamin's position on the aesthetic, arguing that it can have a more productive and pedagogical role. Against a conventional view of aesthetics limited to a depoliticized embrace of formal properties, she championed images that were ugly, destabilizing, and shocking. Such images, argued Sontag, harbor a capacity to show great cruelties precisely in order to arouse compassion and empathy rather than mere titillation. She asserted that "For photographs to accuse, and possibly to alter conduct, they must shock."[27] Shock and rupture become the pedagogical registers of resistance in which the image might talk back to power, unsettling commonsense perceptions while offering "an invitation to pay attention, to reflect, to learn, to examine the rationalizations for mass suffering offered by established powers."[28] Sontag realized that beauty is not always on the side of oppression when presenting images of suffering. Of course, she was just as aware that in a society that makes a spectacle out of violence and human suffering, images that attempt to shock might well reinforce a media-induced comfort with "the horror of certain images."[29]

The Depravity of Aesthetics

The aesthetics of depravity addressed by Sontag, Benjamin, Virilio, and others focuses on suffering through the formal qualities of beauty and design, registering the consumption of images of human pain as a matter of personal pleasure and taste rather than part of a broader engaged social-political discourse. What I call the depravity of aesthetics, by contrast, interprets representations of human suffering, humiliation, and death as part of a wider economy of pleasure that is collectively indulged. This notion of aesthetics focuses on the death drive and how the spectacles of violence that feed it generate a source of gratification and intense socially experienced pleasure. As images of degradation and human suffering become more palatable and pleasurable, the body no longer becomes the privileged space of agency, but "the location of violence, crime, and social pathology."[30] As decadence and despair are normalized in the wider culture—although this is very different from accomplishing their goal to remove all dissent—people are increasingly exploited for their pleasure quotient while any viable notion of the social is subordinated to the violence of a deregulated market economy and its ongoing production of a culture of cruelty.[31]

In this way, representations of human suffering cannot be abstracted from a broader neoliberal regime in which the machinery of consumption endlessly trades in the production of sensationalist images designed to excite, stimulate, and offer the lure of intense sensations. This is especially true for spectacles of violence that are now not only stylistically extraordinary and grotesque, but also grotesque depictions of the culture that produced them. No longer mere bystanders to "every act of violence and violation," the American public eagerly substitutes a pleasure in images of human suffering for any viable sense of moral accountability.[32] How else to explain the insistent demand by many conservative and liberal pundits and the American public at large that the government release the grisly images of Osama bin Laden's corpse, even though the fact of his assassination was never in doubt? How might we understand the growing support among the American populace for state-sanctioned torture and the rising indifference to images that reveal its horrible injustices? Just as torture is sanctioned by the state and becomes normalized for many Americans, the spectacle of violence spreads through the culture with ever greater intensity.

The culture of cruelty runs the gamut of media sources, drenching film and TV screens in lawlessness and fast-paced sledgehammer blood feasts. Violence follows a desperate search for new markets and finds its way into advertisements that sell toys to children, just as it increasingly produces the subject positions and consumer tastes necessary to influence slightly older children. For instance, films such as *Let Me In* (2010), *Hannah* (2011), *Sucker Punch* (2011), and *The Hunger Games* (2012) move from celebrating hyper-violent women to fetishizing hyper-violent young girls.[33] Rather than gain stature through a coming-of-age process that unfolds amid representations of innocence and complicated negotiations with the world, young girls are now valorized for their ability to produce high body counts and their dexterity as killing machines-in-training. Hollywood films such as the *Saw* series, *Inglourious Basterds* (2009), *Zombieland* (2009), *The Killer Inside Me* (2010), and *Scream 4* (2011) all transcend the typical slasher fare and increasingly offer viewers endless, super-charged representations of torture, rape, animal cruelty, revenge, genital mutilation, and much more. Yet another example of such intensely charged images is the recent photo of Lady Gaga posing with a corpse in a sexually suggestive manner.[34] Meanwhile, such images are also saturating the mainstream news, advertising, and much of what circulates online in the United States. Whatever bleeds—now gratuitously and luxuriously—generates profits and dominates media headlines, despite being often presented without any viable context for making sense of the imagery or any critical commentary that might undercut or rupture the pleasure viewers are invited to derive from such images. Representations of violence and human tragedy now merge seamlessly with neoliberalism's culture of cruelty in which risk and mayhem reinforce shared fears rather than shared responsibilities, and a Hobbesian war of all-against-all becomes the organizing principle for structuring a vast array of institutions and social relations.

As corporate capitalism translates into corporate fascism, prominent politicians such as Sarah Palin, radio hosts such as Rush Limbaugh, and media monopoly moguls such as those who deliver Fox News repeatedly deploy the vocabulary of violence to attack the social state, labor unions, immigrants, young people, teachers, and public service employees. At the same time, the depravity of aesthetics gains popular currency in organs of the dominant media that reproduce an endless stream of denigrating images and narratives of people constrained by the forces of poverty, racism, and disability. Their pain and suffering now become a source of delight for late-night comics, radio talk show hosts, and TV programs that provide ample narratives and images of poor families, individuals, and communities who become fodder for the "poverty porn" industry.[35] Programs such as the reality TV series *Jersey Shore*, the syndicated tabloid TV talk show series *The Jerry Springer Show* (and its endless imitators), and *The Biggest Loser* all exemplify what Gerry Mooney and Lynn Hancock claim is a massive "assault on people experiencing poverty [seizing] on any example of 'dysfunctionality' in poor working class communities . . . [exhibiting] expressions of middle-class fears and distrust, [while] also [displaying] a fascination with poverty and the supposedly deviant lifestyles of those affected—where viewers of moral outrage are encouraged to find the worst and weakest moments of people's lives also funny and entertaining."[36]

Spectacles of violence provide an important element in shaping a market-driven culture of cruelty that gives new meaning to the merging of an economy of pleasure and images of violence, mutilation, and human suffering. This is not to suggest that the only images available in contemporary America are those saturated with violence and pain, but to emphasize that the formative culture that produces images that are at odds with, contest, or provide alternatives to such violence seem to be disappearing. Nor am I suggesting that images of violence can only produce an affective economy of sadistic pleasure or be reduced deterministically to one reading and point of view. What I am arguing is that American society—far from being a global democratic leader—has devolved under a neoliberal regime into a media-saturated culture that inordinately invests in and legitimates a grim pleasure in the pain of others, especially those considered marginal and disposable. Decentered and disconnected from any moral criteria, the pleasure-in-death principle, coupled with the search for ever more intense levels of sensation and excitation, becomes the reigning pedagogical and performative force in shaping individual and collective identities.

Within this context, the elevation of cruelty to a structuring principle of society is matched by the privatization of pain, and it is precisely through the depravity of aesthetics that the pleasure of humiliation and violence is maximized.

A carnival of simulated and real violence now produces the depravity of aesthetics in which the culture of cruelty emerges fuelled by a desperate energy and endless menagerie of pain that meld intense excitement with a sense of fulfilment, release, instant arousal, and pleasure. Terry Eagleton comments on the political implications and social costs of this regime of unfettered desires and sensations. He writes, "Sensation in such conditions becomes a matter of commodified shock-value regardless of content: everything can now become pleasure, just as the desensitized morphine addict will grab indiscriminately at any drug. To posit the body and its pleasures as an unquestionably affirmative category is a dangerous illusion, in a social order which reifies and regulates corporeal pleasure for its own ends just as relentlessly as it colonizes the mind."[37]

As the pleasure principle is unconstrained by a moral compass based on a respect for others, it is increasingly shaped by the need for intense excitement and a never-ending flood of heightened sensations. What has led to this immunity and insensitivity to cruelty and prurient images of violence? Part of this process is due to the fact that the American public is bombarded by an unprecedented "huge volume of exposure to . . . images of human suffering."[38] As Zygmunt Bauman argues, there are social costs that come with this immersion of a culture in staged violence. One consequence is that "the sheer numbers and monotony of images may have a 'wearing off' impact [and] to stave off the 'viewing fatigue,' they must be increasingly gory, shocking, and otherwise 'inventive' to arouse any sentiments at all or indeed draw attention. The level of 'familiar' violence, below which the cruelty of cruel acts escapes attention, is constantly rising."[39] Hyper-violence and spectacular representations of cruelty disrupt and block our ability to respond politically and ethically to the violence as it is actually happening on the ground. In this instance, unfamiliar violence such as extreme images of torture and death becomes banally familiar, while familiar violence that occurs daily is barely recognized, becoming, if not boring, then relegated to the realm of the unnoticed and unnoticeable. An increasing volume of violence is pumped into the culture as yesterday's spine-chilling and nerve-wrenching violence loses its shock value. As the need for more intense images of violence accumulates, the moral indifference and desensitization to violence grow while matters of cruelty and suffering are offered up as fodder for sports, entertainment, news media, and other outlets for seeking pleasure.

Cruel acts, while contributing to the further depravity of aesthetics, often escape attention for another reason. With the rise of new and highly advanced computer-generated digital and screen technologies, the space between images and the consequences of real violence becomes more expansive and less meaningful, just as the exercise of real violence becomes easier to perform. Video games, for instance, do more than indulge young participants in cartoonish orgies of violence, slaughter, and mayhem. They are also viewed as a source of valuable training for young twenty-year-olds who are hired by the Defense Department—because of their video game skills—to sit in secluded rooms in California while manipulating drone aircraft designed to target and kill America's enemies in countries such as Iraq, Pakistan, and Afghanistan. Killing in this instance becomes entirely removed from ethical responsibility, while humane actions are reduced to computer errors. Cruelty manifests itself in a depravity that is pleasure-driven and incited by the possibility of a kill, regardless of whether the latter includes innocent victims such as women and children, as often happens in Afghanistan and is portrayed in the now-famous *Collateral Murder* video from Iraq. Released by WikiLeaks, the "graphic video from Baghdad shows a July 2007 attack in which U.S. forces, firing from helicopter gun ships, wounded two children and killed more than a dozen Iraqis, including two Reuters employees."[40] The video verifies the presence of two photographers and a man who, though severely wounded, was later purposely killed along with the civilians who tried to rescue him. The voices of the computer warriors on the tape are merciless, intense, and clearly excited by the pleasure gained from pursuing the targeted and reckless killings.

Under the regime of neoliberal policies, relations, and values, profit-making becomes the only legitimate mode of exchange; private interests replace public concerns; and unbridled individualism infects a society in which the vocabulary of fear, competition, war, and punishment governs existing relationships. Within an economy of pleasure and commodification, freedom is subsumed by a calculated deficit that reduces agency to a regressive infantilism and degraded forms of gratification. What Leo Lowenthal called "the atomization of the individual" bespeaks a figure now terrorized by other human beings and reduced to living "in a state of stupor, in a moral coma."[41] This type of depoliticized inward thinking—with its repudiation of the obligations of shared sociality, disengagement from moral responsibility, and outright disdain for those who are disadvantaged by virtue of being poor, young, or elderly—does more than fuel the harsh, militarized, and ultra-masculine logic of the news and entertainment sector. This "atomization of the individual" also elevates death over life, selfishness over compassion, and economics over politics. The spectrum of disdain and vulnerability has been extended at the current historical moment to contempt for life itself. Life reduced to "bare life" and the vulnerability it produces elicits imperviousness at best, and a new kind of pleasure at worst. Precarity, uncertainty, and misfortune no longer evoke compassion but rather disdain, while simultaneously opening up a space in which vulnerability offers a pretext for forms of pleasure that reinforce a culture of cruelty.[42] But even more so, neoliberal capitalism produces a kind of dysfunctional silence in American society in the face of widespread hardship and suffering—virtually wiping out society's collective memories of moral decency and mutuality.

Aesthetics as both a normative and a performative practice is now enlisted as part of an entertainment–amusement complex. The "cultural apparatus," as C. Wright Mills called it, no longer merely traffics between culture and authority.[43] This apparatus and its public pedagogy now seduce Americans, although not unproblematically, through both a new register and economy of pleasure and a machinery of affect rooted in the spectacle of hyper-violence. Victims no longer have to be looked in the eye because they often appear as just dots on an electronic screen. Staged violence is now anticipated with bated breath by audiences who all too willingly displace moral criteria with "the aesthetically spaced world, structured by the relevancies of [intense excitement], pleasure-potential, [and] interest arousal."[44] One consequence is that a "thick" world of agents, and thus of resistant otherness, is dissolved into a depthless world of gratification, a world that is devoid of opposition.

Neoliberalism's embrace of a "there is no society" ethic is directly related to a diminishing sense of social responsibility. It promotes a kind of individualism that has become pathological in its disdain for community, social values, public life, and the public good.

In a social order marked by the production of atomized, competitive, and militarized subjects, the depravity of

CHAPTER 1

aesthetics aids in the development of a formative culture of social pathology in which individuals are addicted to the pleasure principle now fused with the death drive. Their entwined expression is increasingly circulated and mediated through ever-growing spectacles of violence that feed into a narcissistic and over-the-top consumerist society. As the social state disappears, critical public spheres are commodified, militarized, and hollowed out. One consequence is that democratic institutions, values, and social relations begin to disappear. Under such circumstances, the aesthetics of depravity is reconfigured, transformed into a depravity of aesthetics, thereby relinquishing any power to rupture, transform, enlighten, and critically inform consciousness. Tied to forms of pleasurable consumption and sensations that delight in images of suffering, the depravity of aesthetics functions to anaesthetize ethically and politically, prompting passivity or even joy in the "face of trauma and injustice."[45] As a result, the marriage of pleasure and depravity should not be seen as the province of individual pathology; rather, it serves in the production of a collective subject through an economy of affect that traps people in their own narcissistic desires, aestheticizes violence, and promotes an endless spectacle of shock images. The depravity of aesthetics not only offers the lure of instant personal gratification, but also conceals a hidden order of politics that harbors a deep disdain for social responsibility, justice, and democracy. What is it about the depravity of aesthetics that reveals the smear of the pornographic, a titillation grounded in maximizing the pleasure of violence? What are the political, economic, and social forces bearing down on American society that so easily undercut its potential to raise critical questions about war, violence, morality, and human suffering? How is it that education can so easily be commodified and turned into a spectacle of violence and a source of gruesome entertainment? How is it that under a neoliberal regime of disciplinary power and privatized modes of looking, death and violence can be so easily removed from a critical act of bearing witness? How is it that the very category of the aesthetic is reconstituted as part of a wider circuit of consumption and spectacle of violence, transformed in the end into a depravity of aesthetics?

This is not to suggest that aesthetic standards and values don't matter but to inquire how they come to function in the broader culture. I am not suggesting that the symbiosis of the pleasure principle, the death drive, and the spectacle suggests once and for all that any consideration of aesthetics simply adds insult to the portrayal of human suffering and thus has no place in an emancipatory notion of politics. Photographers, as Mieke Bal points out, "can deploy art not only as a reflection but also as a form of witnessing that alters the existence of what it witnesses."[46] Bal also insists that art can be used "to reconquer beauty [when] mobilized as a weapon *against* suffering," as represented by Nan Goldin's deeply personal photographs displaying the violence and aggression that marked her relationship with her lover. What is at stake with the rise of the depravity of aesthetics—which offers up representations of human suffering, pain, and death as the ultimate repository of desire and pleasure—is not so much the beginning of a debate on the relevance of the aesthetic as much as a dialogue on the limits of the social and the perversion of a formative culture that renders the democratic social impossible while also producing a depravity of aesthetics. This latter line of thought raises a different set of questions. What forms of responsibility and what pedagogical strategies does one invoke in the face of a society that feeds off spectacles of violence and cruelty? What forms of witnessing and education might be called into play in which the feelings of pleasure mobilized by images of human suffering can be used as "a catalyst for critical inquiry and deep thought?"[47] Responding to these questions would mean not only refusing to allow images to dissolve into a neoliberal pleasure machine by interrogating the crimes they portray, but also recognizing, resisting, and transforming the pedagogical function of a cultural apparatus that seriously limits and undermines any viable notion of aesthetics that might extend rather than shut down critical thought, agency, and action in the service of a democracy to come.

Rather than being reduced to a mechanism for the cathartic release of pleasure, a society saturated in the claims of violence, aggression, war, and poisonous modes of masculinity must serve as an indictment, a source of memory, and evidence of the need to imagine otherwise. In pointing to the emerging culture of cruelty, I don't want to suggest that because neoliberal social formations appear to be winning in the United States they have won or that the struggle is over. I think it is too easy to slide from an analysis of such dominant forces to erasing the important issue that this is a struggle, however uneven, that operates within a number of different contexts and is ongoing. In drawing attention to the depravity of aesthetics, I am not arguing that such a project or social formation has achieved domination or is an accomplished and sutured fact of existence, thereby making it easier to ignore how it is located within complex and ongoing spheres of struggle. As Larry Grossberg has pointed out, "The fact that one can read for example a culture of cruelty off of various articulations, does not yet mean that this is how people live their lives. The fact that the cultural discourses are all about markets does not mean that people live their lives with markets as the only definition/locus of value."[48] Indeed, new social formations simultaneously emerge within and across diverse contexts, and we need a new language for describing the nature of such struggles, the complexity of such efforts, and the diverse terrains on which they operate. We need not merely a new language for understanding the many social, political, and cultural formations produced by neoliberalism, but also the ability to understand how neoliberalism and authoritarian political regimes are being challenged by students, workers, and other groups around the world. It is to these formations that I want to briefly turn in order to connect the political and cultural apparatuses of neoliberal violence with the role that higher education might play in learning from wider resistance movements and redefining its role as a democratic public sphere.

Images of Resistance

The youth revolts in the Middle East and Western Europe are not simply a refusal on the part of young people to be written out of the future, but also a rewriting of politics itself. Young people have taken the lead in rejecting a future that for the past thirty years or more has been shamelessly mortgaged by Western countries embracing a form of zombie politics and economic Darwinism, on the one hand, and authoritarian societies in the Middle East that exhibit a deep hatred for democracy, on the other. What is remarkable about the mass revolts in Europe and the Middle East is their demonstration that if young people are granted the time, resources, and support to develop new models of association, then these models will have a better chance at creating the conditions for a future that makes good on the ideals and promises of democratization.

For youth in the United States, whose protests appear less widespread, linked, and sustained, a critical question must be posed. In American society what sort of conditions have young people inherited that obstruct and possibly even undermine their ability to be critical agents capable of waging a massive protest movement against the growing injustices they face on a daily basis? The inability both to be critical of such injustices and to relate them to a broader understanding of politics suggests a failure to think outside of the normative sensibilities of a neoliberal ideology that isolates knowledge and normalizes its own power relations. In fact, one recent study found that even among youth who access higher education "45 percent of students show no significant improvement in the key measures of critical thinking, complex reasoning, and writing by the end of their sophomore years."[49] It is becoming increasingly evident that the corporatization and militarization of schooling over the past few decades have produced a culture of illiteracy and intensified forms of political disengagement. The forms of instrumental training on offer undermine, for example, any critical capacity on the part of students to connect the exorbitant tuition fees they pay to the fact that the United States puts more money into the funding of war, armed forces, and military weaponry than the next twenty-five countries combined—money that could otherwise fund higher education.[50] It has become more difficult for students to recognize how their education in the broadest sense has been systematically devalued, and how this not only undercuts their ability to be engaged critics but contributes further to making American democracy dysfunctional. The value of knowledge is now linked to a crude instrumentalism, and the only mode of education that seems to matter is one that enthusiastically endorses learning marketable skills, embracing a survival-of-the-fittest ethic, and defining the good life solely through accumulation and disposal of the latest consumer goods.

On a global scale, young people, educators, and others who occupy the liminal space of political resistance are now struggling to make official power visible, especially in terms of the toll it takes on those who are viewed as excess, unworthy of government supports, and often excluded from the benefits of a good life. What is being learned from the global struggles is "the idea that people can control the functioning of society [and that] people should make decisions about all the issues that affect them."[51] It is crucial for progressives and others to struggle to create those formative cultures that enable people to translate private injustices into social and systemic problems. At stake here is a notion of democracy that refuses to be reduced to the dictates of a market society. Such a view is crucial for those emergent social movements and struggles that suggest that democracy is once again being viewed as the "sharing of an existence that makes the political possible."[52] Hopefully what we will see from those fighting the nightmare of neoliberalism is a narrative of both critique and possibility, one that reclaims the public conversation about memory as a condition for learning, higher education as a crucial public good, academics as public intellectuals, and critical agency as a basis for engaged citizenship.

In contrast to the banally grotesque images circulated by the U.S. public pedagogy machine, we have seen Arendt's "instants of truth" in images from Libya, Syria, and Iran in which the murders of a young student and other protesters by state militia thugs have been captured on video and circulated the world over. The video images of the killing of a young twenty-seven-year-old music student, Neda Agha Soltan, helped to inspire massive waves of protests in Iran that continue to this day. Similarly, terrifying images of the torture and killing of thirteen-year-old Hamza Ali al-Khateeb have spread throughout Syria to indict the state security forces who murdered him. Such images in these countries become a pedagogical tool, a critical mode of public pedagogy capable of forms of witnessing that allow people to imagine the unimaginable. What is emancipatory about these images, as Georges Didi-Huberman points out in a different context, is that they work to refuse what he calls the "disimagination machine"; that is, these are images that are "images in spite of all"—bearing witness to a different and critical sense of remembering, agency, ethics, and collective resistance.[53] These images have ignited massive collective protests against repressive governments. Such images did not feed the basest of collective desires and pleasurable fantasies detached from any real consequences. To the contrary, such images of abuse and suffering have inflamed a society in which a formative culture exists that enables people to connect emotional investments and desires to a politics in which unthinkable acts of violence are confronted as part of a larger "commitment to political accountability, community, and the importance of positive affect for both belonging and change."[54]

If young people in the United States do not yet display a strong commitment to democratic politics and collective struggle, it is because they have lived through thirty years of "a debilitating and humiliating disinvestment in their future," especially if they are marginalized by class, ethnicity, and race.[55] The assault on higher education in the United States, while not as severe as in Europe, still suggests ample reasons for students to be in the streets protesting against such policies. Nearly forty-three states have pledged major cuts to higher education in order to compensate for insufficient state funding. This means an unprecedented hike in tuition rates is being implemented; enrollments are being slashed; salaries are being reduced; and in some states need-based scholarships are being eliminated. Pell Grants, which allow poor students to attend college, are being cut. Robert Reich has chronicled some of the effects on university budgets, which include the following: Georgia cutting "state funding for higher education by $151 million"; Michigan reducing "student financial aid by $135 million";[56] Florida raising tuition in its eleven public universities by 15 percent; and the University of California increasing tuition by 40 percent in two years.[57] As striking as these increases are, tuition has steadily risen over the past several decades, becoming a disturbingly normative feature of post-secondary education. Millions of students pass through the halls of higher education in the United States. It is crucial that they be educated in ways that enable them to recognize the poisonous forces of corporatization and militarization and their effects throughout American society. Particularly important is the capability to understand how these effects threaten "democratic government at home just as they menace the independence and sovereignty of other countries."[58] Both students and the larger public must be alerted to the ways in which the military–industrial–academic complex has restructured higher education so as to dismantle it as a place in which to think critically, imagine otherwise, and engage in modes of knowledge production and research that address pressing social problems and encourage students to participate in public debate and civic engagement.[59] This role of higher education is especially crucial at a time when, as Frank Rich has pointed out, "We live in a culture where accountability and responsibility are forgotten values."[60]

But there is more at stake here than educating students to be alert to the dangers of militarization and the ways in which it is infiltrating popular culture as well as redefining the very mission of higher education. Critics such as David Price, the late Chalmers Johnson, Sheldon Wolin, Nick Turse, and Andrew Bacevich have convincingly argued that if the United States is to avoid degenerating into a military dictatorship, a grassroots movement will have to occupy center stage in opposing militarization, government secrecy, and imperial power, while reclaiming the basic principles of democracy.[61] This means rejecting the established political parties; forming alternative, democratic, anti-militarization movements; and developing the groundwork for long-term organizations, new solidarities, and social movements to resist the growing ties among higher education, the armed forces, intelligence agencies, and the war industries—ties that play a crucial role in reproducing militarized knowledge.

The spectacle of terror and raw violence as entertainment along with the conditions that have produced it do not sound the death knell of democracy, but demand that we "begin to rethink democracy from within these conditions."[62] How might we construct a cultural politics based on social relations that enable individuals and social groups to rethink the crucial nature of pedagogy, agency, and social responsibility in a violence-saturated global public sphere? How can we begin to address old and new media technologies within a democratic cultural politics that challenges religious fundamentalism, neoliberal ideology, militarization, and the cult of mindless violent entertainment? Such a collective project requires a politics that is in the process of being invented, one that has to be attentive to the new realities of power, global social movements, and the promise of a planetary democracy. At stake here are both modes of critical education and public spheres that develop those modes of knowledge and skills needed to critically understand the new visual and visualizing technologies and their attendant screen culture, not simply as new modes of communication, but as structural forces and educational tools capable of expanding critical citizenship, animating public life, and extending democratic public spheres.

Roger Simon has suggested that there is a need for various individuals and groups to develop pedagogical practices that encourage a form of attentiveness that enables audiences to engage in a dialogue with the stories told by spectacles of terror and fear, regardless of their source.[63] Such a pedagogy would reject the anti-intellectualism, the fear of critical dialogue, and the general indifference to the stories of others that are embedded in the pedagogy of the violent spectacle. In addressing what kind of pedagogical work is performed by the spectacle of terror and the culture of depravity, audiences would analyze, first, how their own gaze might be aligned with the insidious modes and bodies of power that participate in images of destruction, humiliation, and fear; and, second, what is at stake in their attraction, expanding upon the highly individuated response solicited by the neoliberal spectacle. The experience of the spectacle, the culture of market-driven violence, and the disdain for critical thought that drives the current historical conjuncture must be critically examined by analyzing the power relations and institutions that make up its social networks and modes of storytelling. Crucial here is how the neoliberal-driven spectacle works to eliminate memory and reduce public issues to private concerns. How do neoliberalism and the formative culture that supports it, whether in the world of film, television, newspapers, the Internet, or other forms of public pedagogy, undercut those modes of power, contexts, and relations that can address a public rather than a merely private sensibility? Neoliberalism and the spectacle of terror resonate with the entrenched spirit of social Darwinism, while simultaneously impoverishing higher education and other public spheres that demand democratic modes of subjectivity and sociality. Neoliberalism's culture of cruelty, consumption, and terror paralyzes critical agency through the regressive retreat into privatized worries and fears, and powerfully undermines all notions of dialogue, critical engagement, and historical remembrance.[64] Against such a spectacle, there is the need for modes of critical education and social movements that value a culture of questioning, view critical agency as a condition of public life, and reject voyeurism in favor of the search for justice.

Neoliberalism's end point merges a culture of cruelty with a depravity of aesthetics, both of which envelop our lives through a vast array of technologies ranging from smart phones to computers to televisions, all inextricably linked to how we understand ourselves and our relationship to others within a democratic global public sphere. But neoliberalism also contributes to policies such as the racist laws being enacted in Arizona and other states, which exemplify the power of fear and the appeal to terror to short-circuit any sense of reason, justice, and freedom. The cultural front is one of our most important pedagogical sites and it must be rethought, appropriated, and used to reject the dystopian, anti-intellectual, and often racist vision at work in the spectacle of terror and culture of fear and, in doing so, provide a language of both criticism and hope as a condition for rethinking the possibilities of the future and the promise of global democracy itself.

If higher education is to come to grips with the multilayered pathologies produced by neoliberalism and its formative culture of cruelty and militarization of everyday life, students, faculty, and others will have to rethink both the space of the university as a democratic public sphere and the global spaces and public spheres in which intellectuals, educators, students, artists, labor unions, and other social actors and movements can form transnational alliances to oppose the death-dealing ideology of militarization and its effects on the world. These effects include violence, pollution, massive poverty, racism, the arms trade, growth of privatized armies, civil conflict, child slavery, and the ongoing wars in Iraq and Afghanistan. True to the logic of privatization, private companies now offer military services for hire, treating their products as any other commodity for sale.[65] As the Obama regime embraces the policies of the military–industrial–academic complex with unbridled fervor, it is time for educators and students to take a stand and develop global organizations that can be mobilized in the effort to supplant a culture of war with a culture of peace whose elemental principles must be grounded in relations of economic, political, cultural, and social justice and the desire to sustain human life. This is as much a pedagogical task as it is a political project.

2

Venture Philanthropy and the Neoliberal Assault on Public Education

Kenneth J. Saltman

Educational philanthropy has been recently remade on the model of venture capital. This is part of the broader neoliberal remaking of public education that most significantly advances a privatization and deregulation agenda. Venture philanthropists in education, including the Gates, Broad, and Walton Foundations, have been pushing vouchers, charter schools, scholarship tax credits (neovouchers) and funding the infrastructure of the school privatization movement, from think tanks and lobbying groups to political organizations to scholarship and publicity to grassroots "Astroturf" campaigns. As well, the venture philanthropists are behind the expansion of standardized test-based measures of educational value, attempts to transform educational leadership and teacher education in anti-intellectual and anti-critical formats, and the modeling of reform on corporate culture and ideals.

Although educational philanthropy and venture philanthropy in particular represent a very small portion of the roughly $600 billion annual expenditure on education in the United States, venture philanthropy has a strategic aim of leveraging private money to influence public schooling in ways compatible with the following: long-standing privatization agendas of the political Right; conservative think tanks such as the Heritage Foundation, the Hoover Institution, and the Fordham Foundation; corporate foundations such as ExxonMobil; and corporate organizations such as the Business Roundtable and the Commercial Club of Chicago. The central agenda is to transform public education in the United States into a market through for-profit and nonprofit charter schools, vouchers, and "scholarship" tax credits for private schooling, or "neovouchers." Venture philanthropies such as New Schools Venture Fund and the Charter School Growth Fund are being financed by the large givers and aim to create national networks of charter schools, charter management organizations, and educational management organizations (EMOs). These organizations are explicit about their intent to radically transform public education in the United States through various strategies. Working along these lines, the venture philanthropists also coordinate with large urban school districts and business groups to orchestrate such plans as New York's New Visions for Public Schools, Chicago's Renaissance 2010, and similar mixed-income schools and housing projects in Portland, OR, Boston, MA, and elsewhere. These organizations coordinate the privatizations of schooling and housing and gentrify coveted sections of cities. They aggressively seek to reimagine teacher education through corporate-based online and onsite initiatives and educational leadership on the model of the MBA. The key players of venture philanthropy in education—including but not limited to such leaders as Gates, Walton, Fisher, and Broad—are able to exercise influence disproportionate to their size and spending power through strategic arrangements with charter and voucher-promoting organizations, think tanks, universities, school districts, and schools. The seed money that underfunded schools desperately seek allows the venture philanthropists to leverage influence over educational policy and planning, curriculum, and instructional practices and influence the very idea of what it means to be an educated person. Although the implications for educational reform are vast, scholarship on venture philanthropy in education has been scant.[1]

In what follows, I first illustrate how the logic and assumptions of "Gatesian" venture philanthropy depart radically from the traditional "scientific" philanthropy typified by Andrew Carnegie that dominated the twentieth century. Venture philanthropy is not merely a reflection of particular values and interests but also functions pedagogically by producing particular ideas and ideologies about educational obligation in a highly privatized way. Of chief interest is the question of why educational philanthropy serves capital interests differently in the age of scientific philanthropy as opposed to the age of venture philanthropy. I then discuss how venture philanthropy needs to be understood as part of what I have termed "Education as Enforcement," which examines the intersections of the corporatization and militarization of schooling and society. This section elaborates on the ways that class and cultural power are wielded through schooling designed to enforce neoliberalism. The next section emphasizes how venture philanthropy and neoliberal educational reform succeed in part by making consumerist promises grounded in a logic of educational exchange. I conclude by suggesting a notion of educational exchange based in universal obligation and critical forms of educational projects and activism that can counter the neoliberal educational agenda and instead foster critical democratic forms of schooling and contribute to broader egalitarian transformation.

From Traditional to Venture Philanthropy

Venture philanthropy differs markedly from prior educational philanthropy, dominant throughout the twentieth century, that included large donors such as The Carnegie Corporation, The Rockefeller Foundation, and The Ford Foundation. These traditional philanthropic endeavors were defined by a sense of the public obligation of industrialists to give back some of the surplus wealth that they had accumulated. Carnegie's *The Gospel of Wealth* codifies this perspective that its advocates described as scientific philanthropy.

As critics such as Robert Arnove, Joan Roelofs, and others have argued, the early educational philanthropy played the distinctly conservative cultural role of supporting public institutions in ways compatible with the ideological perspectives and material interests of the captains of industry rather than those of the workers of coal, steel, oil, or automotive production. Such labor created the surplus wealth that then went into educational institutions, museums, libraries, and trusts. Public subsidies through tax incentives not only encouraged but financed such public works to be developed and designed by fiscal and cultural elites rather than by the broader public.

Although educational philanthropy played a hegemonic role throughout the twentieth century, it was hardly unified in its approaches and offered funding for a wide variety of initiatives and projects that were not restricted to the conservative side of the political spectrum. There was a distance between the donors and the uses made of the money in education. "Scientific philanthropy," though beholden to the logic of cultural imperialism,[2] was marked by a spirit of public obligation and deeply embedded in a liberal democratic ethos.

Venture philanthropy departs radically from the age of scientific industrial philanthropy. Venture philanthropy is modeled on venture capital, in particular, its investments in the technology boom of the early 1990s. Venture philanthropy is consistent with both the upward material distributions of a "new Gilded Age" and the steady expansion of neoliberal language and rationales in public education, including the increasing centrality of business terms to describe educational reforms and policies: choice, competition, efficiency, accountability, monopoly, turnaround, and failure. Likewise, venture philanthropy treats giving to public schooling as a "social investment" that, like venture capital, must begin with a business plan, involve quantitative measurement of efficacy, be replicable to be "brought to scale," and that ideally will leverage public spending in ways compatible with the strategic donor. Grants are referred to as "investments," donors are called "investors," impact is renamed "social return," evaluation becomes "performance measurement," grant-reviewing turns into "due diligence," the grant lists are renamed "investment portfolios," and charter networks are referred to as "franchises," to name just some of the remodeling of giving on investment and particularly on venture capital models.

Within the view of venture philanthropy, donors are framed in private terms as both entrepreneurs and consumers, while recipients are represented as investments. One of the most significant aspects of this transformation in educational philanthropy involves the ways in which the public and civic purposes of public schooling are re-described by venture philanthropy in distinctly private ways. Such a view carries significant implications for a society dedicated to public democratic ideals. This is no small matter in terms of how the public and civic roles of public schooling have become nearly overtaken by the economistic neoliberal perspective that views public schooling as principally a matter of producing workers and consumers for the economy and for global economic competition.[3] Rather than breaking with the neoliberal economic assumptions about education that intensified throughout the Reagan, Bush, Clinton, and Bush years, the Obama administration displays a deep commitment to expanding radically the twin imperatives of neoliberal education in the form of privatization and deregulation: charter schooling (despite a lack of compelling evidence for its boasted successes); implementing Wall Street–style bonuses tied to test scores for teachers and students; pushing urban education projects, such as those in Chicago and New

Orleans, that are tied to public housing privatization and destruction and that dispossess citizens of their communities while de-unionizing school districts and maintaining racial segregation.[4] The local business groups that coordinate with venture philanthropists push such neoliberal urban education reform initiatives.

The Uses of Scientific Philanthropy

A leading scholar on philanthropy, Stanley Katz specifies the particularly public understanding held by early-twentieth-century leaders of scientific philanthropy. "I want to use the term 'philanthropy' in the special sense originated by Carnegie and the senior Rockefeller: the self-conscious donation of truly large sums of private wealth to do public good by addressing the causes (and also manifestations) of social problems of all kinds."[5] It should be said from the outset here that for critics on the Left, the causes of social problems are the social structures and systems that facilitate the vast amassing of wealth by few at the expense of many. The projects of Carnegie and Rockefeller were defined through the public interest and appear on one level to be concerned with redistributive efforts toward ameliorating inequalities in wealth and income as well as intertwined cultural inequalities such as unequal access to education. However, as Katz, among others, points out, the scientific philanthropists were deeply conservative and understood their giving as having a practical use for themselves and others of their class.

Scientific philanthropists sought not simply to use private money for public gain but to serve ruling class interests in a number of ways. These conservative intents include delegitimating socialist politics and movements, establishing institutions that directly serve elites, assuring social reform rather than radical structural change, and creating social networks to secure the status of elites.[6] Additionally, foundations have supported social programs such as Social Security to assuage depression-era labor unrest, and they worked to support tax laws that prohibited giving to political parties. They also provided support for civil rights and minority education projects in part to diffuse minority interest and support for radical movements. Foundations also supported "democracy promotion" projects overseas that would increase the likelihood of political economic formations tending toward liberal capitalism rather than socialism or communism.[7] Carnegie exhorted the super-rich to found universities, and many did, including Cornell, Stanford, Johns Hopkins, and Rockefeller. Stanford and Chicago have been hotbeds of neoliberal thought: the University of Chicago arguably was the birthplace of neoliberalism under Milton Friedman (some would claim London School of Economics and Hayek), and leaders of the push to privatize public schooling are associated with the Hoover Institution housed at Stanford. This is not to say that no progressive or radical political thought has come out of these universities but rather to highlight the centrality of foundations to the early formation of educational policies that have left a conservative legacy.

The scope of liberal and sometimes even progressive commitments to the public sector emerging from scientific philanthropy does not invalidate the conservative project of undermining radical movements for systemic change and genuine democracy, nor does this history invalidate the reality that the commitment to the public good did result in the strengthening of the deliberative aspects of the public sphere. Both aims can be found explicitly stated in Carnegie's *The Gospel of Wealth*. He writes that the best gift philanthropy can give to a community is a free library, "provided the community will accept and maintain it as a public institution, as much a part of the city property as its public schools, and indeed, an adjunct to these." Carnegie emphasized the value to the public of the free access to knowledge and information, and he understood public knowledge institutions as ameliorative by allowing the poor opportunities for self-advancement.

Carnegie, like the leading educationalist of his day, G.

Stanley Hall (who is largely responsible for the late-nineteenth-century field of the study of adolescence), accepts the racially grounded doctrine of recapitulation theory. Recapitulation theory holds that the development of the human being repeats the development of the human race, and that the successful development of the human race toward civilization depends upon youth being forced to undergo the trials of earlier stages of human development. These trials build character in middle-class white boys and prepare them to lead civilization forward.[8] Such movements as scouting and the YMCA typify such early-twentieth-century thinking that viewed getting back to primitive nature as a necessary strengthening endeavor to prepare youth for stewardship of civilization. In the view of recapitulation theory, human development follows from primitive nature to animals to lower humans to higher humans. Within this schema, white European males are at the top of the upward chain of nature. However, white boys, in particular, need to go back down the chain to get toughened up for the stresses of governing advancing civilization. In *The Gospel of Wealth*, Carnegie celebrates his own impoverished childhood and the character he gained by working as a child laborer in the textile industry. He describes his adult visit to the home of a Sioux Indian chief and makes much of the fact that the lowliest Indian and the chief live in indistinguishable dwellings. For Carnegie, this illustrates the superiority of Euro-American civilization. The difference between the worker's cottage and the millionaire's mansion indicates for him an upward movement toward greater and greater civilization. He argues that capitalism raises everybody's quality of life and that the amenities available to the worst-off in civilized society are superior to the living standards of kings in prior eras. However, competition and the refusal of aristocratic inheritance make possible the forward movement toward greater and greater innovation and civilization. Carnegie extols the virtues of poverty and the valuable lessons bestowed upon child laborers, and also laments the misfortune of the children of the rich who do not benefit from the character-building blessing of destitution. Carnegie sees the Sioux as both stuck in the prior history of the human race and as communistic—communism, Carnegie explains, is not progress but regress, bringing humanity back to the life-standards of "primitives." For Carnegie, capitalism produces both wealth and poverty. The dim and stultified aristocrats of old Europe have suffered from the mistake of inheritance. Carnegie exhorts his millionaire contemporaries to be ashamed to die with their wealth. Instead, they ought to give it to the public so that those who can help themselves will do so. Those incapable of helping themselves should be left to the care of the state, he explains.

Central to Carnegie's view of philanthropy is the value of self-help and also the definition of human worth through economic productivity. Carnegie rails against the violence of frivolous giving of charity, suggesting that the nickel given away on the street goes on to do compounded harm to the recipient whose productive energies will be drained by the possibility of unproductive acquisition. Scientific philanthropy for Carnegie must be highly rationalized on the basis of its inspiration for fostering economic productivity. However, it also must contribute to the public good in a way that cannot be strictly reduced to the economic. Indeed, Carnegie has harsh words for the wealthy person who flaunts wealth in conspicuous displays rather than by giving to the public. And Carnegie opposes the giving of vast private inheritances to children, seeing this as a diffusion of productive energies and a corrupting influence. Perhaps what is most significant in Carnegie is the expansion of a perspective toward wealth found in Benjamin Franklin's autobiography. Franklin taught his readers to view money as having a life of its own and a reproductive capacity. The squandering of wealth was akin to killing productive offspring. Of course, both Franklin's and Carnegie's view of wealth, as being strictly guided by rational utility, typifies the increased rationalization of giving in accord with capitalism.[9] Carnegie's vision for philanthropy deeply displaced a value on dispensing wealth and marked a turn toward the shift from *charity* to *philanthropy*. Bill Gates and other venture philanthropists mark another significant shift in the western understanding of giving.

Bill Gates read Carnegie in preparation for establishing his Bill and Melinda Gates Foundation. There are certain elements of Carnegie's thought that Gates continues, including the rationalization of philanthropy as necessarily fostering "productive" individuals and greasing the inclusion of working people in the ideologies of a corporate-dominated economy that mostly undermines their own interests. However, there are numerous glaring differences between the social visions of Carnegie and Gates. Carnegie viewed public schools and public libraries as being crucial for making knowledge and information freely available to individuals. While Carnegie idealized hard work, self-improvement, and self-reliance despite potentially punishing economic and material conditions, it was the publicly and freely supported immaterial labor (self-education) that the individual could pursue for self-improvement and economic advancement. For Carnegie, while the public sector should certainly not redistribute access to public control over capital, the public sector should make freely available the means for individual access to information that would benefit the individual and contribute to the making of a more educated workforce and informed citizenry. On the contrary, Bill Gates earned his historically unmatched fortune specifically by using intellectual property laws to own, control, and license the products of immaterial labor, namely software and digital information. That is, Gates's wealth is principally the result not of the sharing and free exchange of knowledge in the public domain, celebrated as the route to freedom and a democratic public by Carnegie, but rather is a product of the restriction and commodification of knowledge. In the 1970s, computer hobbyists freely shared their hardware and software innovations in a kind of hippie-tech movement. Some of the software that would go on to result in spectacular profits for Microsoft, Apple, and other computer companies began as freely shared innovations by hobbyists. Gates and Steve Jobs, among other early leaders of the nascent computer industry, were particularly adept at commercializing and monopolizing the innovations of others.[10] In fact, what would come to be called shareware or open source software is closer to the spirit of the early software and computer innovators who were motivated less by the potential for profits than they were by intellectual curiosity, the technology itself, and the challenges of solving problems.

While Carnegie eschewed conspicuous displays of wealth and excessive consumption, Gates champions a version of schooling that idealizes a corporate economy in which consumer spending on manufactured needs is at the core. So, venture philanthropy intensifies the economic rationalization of giving by insisting that giving be more tightly controlled, especially in terms of its outcomes. Yet it also departs from the ties that scientific philanthropy had to the ideals of a productive industrial economy. In a sense, the transformation of philanthropy reflects the transformation in the understanding of productivity and utility accompanying the shift in the United States from an industrial to a consumer and service-based economy. To put it differently, as the core of the economy has become increasingly defined by the imperative for economic growth that depends on ever more frivolous consumer spending and the fabrication of ever new irrational consumer needs and desires, unplanned and unrationalized giving appears increasingly as a problem in need of eradication. One way to think about this is that as squandering and irrational expenditure of energy, wealth, and resources is increasingly central to economic growth in a consumer society, squandering and irrational expenditure, like the giving of charity, appear increasingly as a problem, and it must be rationalized and expressed through authorized, legitimate, planned, and orderly forms. Charity must appear as investment. The logic of this creeping rationalization in the irrational consumer economy is particularly evident in the aesthetic realm. The value and celebration of utility, the display of usefulness, can be seen, for example, in the long-standing popularity (from the early 1990s to the present) of the SUV, in which the individual sporting (display) of potential usefulness is both a kind of status and carries with it a moralism about excessive expenditure—the luxury car is decadent, but such decadence is acceptable when in the form of a useful truck. Of course in reality, what could be a more frivolous expenditure than using a large gas-guzzling truck to run errands around town? This became obvious only when the price of gas radically spiked to more than $4 per gallon in a short span of time in 2008.

In the next two sections, I highlight the threats to critical, public, and democratic values posed by neoliberal educational reform, and then I ask what is being promised through it.

Education as Enforcement: The Threats of Neoliberal Education

In 2003, David Gabbard and I published a co-edited collection called *Education as Enforcement: The Militarization and Corporatization of Schools*. When the first edition of *Education as Enforcement* was edited, the United States, with more than a hundred permanent military bases around the globe, was a nation at war in Afghanistan. As the second edition went to print in 2010, the United States had been at war on two fronts for eight years, with high troop levels expected in Iraq indefinitely and the war in Afghanistan escalated by a president who campaigned on ending the war in Iraq and who (in the tradition of Kissinger who also won the Peace Prize before escalating the Vietnam War) gave a Nobel Peace Prize speech defending his war escalation. Entering first-year university students in the United States in 2010–2011 will have spent about half of their lives living in a nation at war and will have experienced the events of 9/11 as children. These facts illustrate the extent to which the waging of war has become a kind of natural social fact, a backdrop for life in the United

States, but also at the same time something largely kept out of the consciousness and experience of most American citizens' daily lives. Most citizens are educated heavily by infotainment, advertising, and public relations, a steady stream of celebrity-oriented trivia and gossip. Despite being awash in unlimited information that they could use to participate in democratic public life, they are largely produced not as participating citizens but rather principally as consumers and spectators. The central concern of the book remains the ways that schooling and other educative forces undermine the conditions for public and critical forms of democracy.

The first edition of *Education as Enforcement* was a successful book in part because it spoke to dramatic transformations in schools and society in a timely way. Since that publication, the militarization of schools, the corporatization of schools, and significant anti-democratic trends have all dramatically increased. The militarization of schools has expanded most notably through the increasing efforts to open JROTC programs across the United States; the ongoing cultural pedagogies of mass media that educate children and adults to identify with militaristic, authoritarian, and anti-democratic practices; the expansion of public schools run as military academies; the expansion of the troops to teachers program; and the expansion of military leaders idealized as school leaders. Critics and activists continue to point out that many of these programs (especially JROTC and military academies) aggressively target poor and working class youth of color for military recruitment and deny high-quality public schooling to these students, and then offer instead military educations, fail to address the sexual orientation discrimination in the military and its incompatibility with the anti-discrimination demands of public schooling, and expand into public schooling deeply conservative values including militarism, patriarchy, and hierarchical and authoritarian social relations.

In the past decade, public schools have been converted into military academies as both stand-alone schools and as "carve outs" of existing schools. Chicago leads the nation both with the most JROTC programs and with the most public schools run as military academies. Intersecting with neoliberal "choice" initiatives, these academies offer a military education to students who are otherwise offered severely underfunded public schools. Rather than investing in improving public schools, such choice schemes hold students hostage to versions of schooling that, for example, teach science and mathematics through naval warfare. These schools receive funding from both traditional sources and the U.S. Department of Defense.

Shortly before the first edition of *Education as Enforcement*, the United States had begun significantly militarizing civil society with the USA Patriot Act, the erosion of *posse commitatus*, the replacement of judicial process by military tribunal, the legal and cultural justification of torture as a tool of state policy, the military recruitment of youth, and the transformation of schools into military academies. The United States and corporate media had also begun a cultural pedagogical project in which a spectacle of jingoistic patriotism and the terrorism alleged to justify it merged with a fanatical defense of "our way of life," defined by the endless expansion of consumerism and corporate wealth concentration backed by neoliberal ideology and its market fundamentalism.

As the introduction to the first edition suggested, the book sought to explain the relationship between the expansion of military and corporate language, models, and practices in schools and society. A central connection between these trends is neoliberal ideology. Neoliberalism is an ideology that pushes privatization (the selling off of public institutions to private ownership and control) and deregulation (the redistribution from the public to the private sector controls and limits over trade, investment, and labor) while suggesting that all public goods be understood privately as markets. As Pierre Bourdieu suggested shortly before his death, neoliberalism guts the caregiving role of the state and promotes its repressive roles, especially military and policing. *Education as Enforcement* contends that the crisis of political democracy facing the United States owes in large part to neoliberalism and the end to a "constitutive outside" of liberal capitalism. The sense that there is no alternative to the present other than to enforce the dictates of the capitalist economy was not shaken by the events of 9/11 but rather reinforced with the discourse of national security drastically expanded as a defense of "our way of life." The Bush administration positioned all alternatives to U.S.-style liberal capitalism (or repressive regimes friendly to it) as part of or potentially part of an "axis of evil." Another way to understand this is that the post-9/11 security state marked the project of more aggressively militarizing the integration of the "non-integrating gap." In this sense the pre-9/11 corporate and state ideal of neoliberal globalization was deepened over the first decade of the new century. Yet the neoconservative movement that put George W. Bush in the White House and that sought to expand the nation-state based on unipolar power has resulted, in the words of Giovanni Arrighi, in "hegemony unraveling." The United States is a financially and militarily overextended empire, awash in foreign debt, and using public money to bail out private industry—a kind of socialism for the super-rich. Rather than countering these trends, the Obama administration has largely sought to continue them, assuring that half of the federal budget will go for military spending, escalating military attacks that kill civilians in the Middle East, Asia, and Africa; redistributing wealth upward; and using public wealth to help the richest citizens while ensuring that the reforms to health care, education, and housing remain under corporate control. There are high social costs to the ongoing expansion of militarism, the ongoing culture of neoliberalism, and the repressive and business-framed remaking of public education in the United States. Perhaps most crucially at a moment in history when Americans need a critical vocabulary and the theoretical, historical, ethical, and political tools to interpret and act on the pressing public problems facing the United States and the world, U.S. public schooling is increasingly being remade to remove critical and intellectual practices in favor of scripted lessons, high-stakes testing, "banking education," and approaches to teaching and learning that are effectively prohibitions on thinking.

The corporatization of schooling includes the expansion of for-profit companies running schools (EMOs), for-profit and nonprofit charter schooling, expansion of voucher schemes, and expanded managerialism that imagines schools as businesses, students as consumers of educational services, and parents as shoppers. Within this view, the goal of universal public provision of schooling is replaced with the metaphors of "competition" and "choice." The historical legacy of unequal educational distribution is reinterpreted in this view as a problem with too little market discipline. If only, so goes the thinking, public schools are forced to compete against each other for scarce resources, they will be forced to improve. The assumption in this view is that educational quality is primarily a matter of teacher, student, and administrator indiscipline (a frequently gender- and racially coded accusation) and that corporate reforms can impose the necessary discipline to force everyone to "do their job." This now-prevalent punitive thinking dominates No Child Left Behind (NCLB) and Race to the Top as well as the testing and "value-added" agendas dominating the reform scene. These assumptions misunderstand motivations, presuming that everyone wants primarily to "get away with" not teaching well. In reality, most teachers are motivated by the deep satisfaction they get from students learning and by a passion for what they teach. Most students are motivated by curiosity and fascination when subjects are meaningful. The dominant wrong-headed imperatives of enforcing the "right" knowledge first undermine teaching and learning as intellectual and creative processes of investigation and curiosity. They first kill the passion for learning by making knowledge a dead thing to be consumed. They then blame students and teachers for failing to be excited by dead knowledge rendered meaningless and decontextualized through standardization. An endless series of corporate and military reforms are then brought in to schooling in hopes of enforcing the right knowledge. This enforcement thinking is the problem, not the solution it purports to be. Perhaps most importantly, as knowledge is rendered decontextualized, meaningless, and ossified, students are hindered from comprehending knowledge in relation to broader public matter and social problems, the experiences of daily life, and the structures of power informing those experiences.

Educational policy makers, politicians across political parties, think tanks, and mass media continue to accept the neoliberal view that schooling should principally serve the needs of business to make future consumers and workers while undercutting the crucial democratic role schools play in preparing citizens for active self-governance. Such preparation requires that students develop the critical tools to interpret and act collectively on public problems. Yet the corporate school reforms of measuring learning largely through standardized tests, teacher and student cash for grades and scores, private contracting, and heavy reliance on for-profit textbook and testing all promote conceptions of learning that shut down the most crucial critical questions: Whose version of truth is put forward and why? What is the relationship between claims to truth and claims to social authority? What historical and social conditions give rise to particular claims to truth? How are claims to truth related to broader social forces and struggles? How are particular bodies of knowledge valued relative to others?

In the first eight years of the new millennium, massive tax cuts for the rich, slashed social spending, and deregulating markets to permit reckless speculation allowed concentrations of wealth to reach unprecedented levels in the United States, described by some as a second Gilded Age. Neoliberalism, as David Harvey aptly explains in *A Brief History of Neoliberalism*,[11] has been a project of class warfare waged by the rich on everyone else. Neoliberal educational reform is no exception to this, aiming to turn public schools into private investment, to treat schooling as a private consumable commodity, and to gut the democratic, critical, and public aspects of education to make docile "disciplined" subjects through high-stakes testing, standardization of curriculum, and attacks on teacher work, while imagining schools as businesses that should be run by "bullish CEOs" drawn from the military and the corporate sector.

The role of public education within this dominant view has intensified since 1983's *A Nation at Risk* report, which at the outset of the neoliberal "Reagan Revolution" recast education as a matter of military and economic competition. Schools are to create foremost consumers and workers who can contribute to global economic competition for the nation. National security in this view is a matter of the health of the corporate economy and its capacity to maintain ever greater spending on military contracting to project the power of the one superpower and enforce global order in a form acceptable to U.S. interests (capital). In 2008, the United States spent a total of about a trillion dollars on education, but the U.S. federal government contributes only about 8 percent of education spending. In contrast, U.S. military spending, which is largely all federal, ran about $700 billion in 2008. In that year, the United States accounted for 48 percent of total world military spending. The United States also remains year after year one of the top sellers of weapons to other countries around the world. The United States wields power through repressive force by maintaining the world's largest prison system by far, with 1 in 100 Americans living incarcerated as of 2009 and with for-profit prisons and juvenile detention growing as industries.

Despite escalating military engagement, the neoconservative dream of a unipolar superpower has unraveled. It has become evident that the United States cannot afford to assert nation-state-based imperial aggression indefinitely. With the financial crisis of 2008 and the massive state intervention to save Wall Street, the basic tenets of neoliberal economic doctrine (unfettered deregulation and privatization) have been largely discredited as well. Yet, in education, neoliberal assumptions are being aggressively pursued across the political spectrum in multiple forms of privatization, deregulation, managerialism, and union-busting, as well as resurgent positivism. Militarizing schools and civil society is not principally what keeps Americans consenting to or even supporting policies hostile to public forms of democratic life. Instead, it is the cultural pedagogies of mass media that play a crucial role in educating citizens by producing identifications and subject positions conducive to violent, militarized, and destructively market-based solutions to social problems. As the collapse of neoliberal economic tenets and the failure of military solutions to global problems illustrate, these anti-democratic approaches are utterly unsustainable both economically and ecologically. Nonetheless, these are precisely the values pushed aggressively by the venture philanthropists.

What exactly is *promised* by venture philanthropy and neoliberal educational reform more generally?

The "Promise" of Neoliberal Educational Reform

Neoliberal educational reform promises the student the dream world of consumer luxury found in a consumer society—a promise that dominates educational policy. The call and implementation of high-stakes standardized testing, the standardization of curriculum, the vocationalization of schooling, hyper-rationalization of all aspects of schooling, the calls to treat public schooling like a market—all of these are justified as leading to the promise of greater and greater consumption. The promise is based on educational exchange. The individual who works hard learning that which others have determined is important is ultimately promised the exchange of grades for higher schooling, and then promised the exchange of grades and graduation for work, then promised the exchange of work for greater income, and ultimately promised the ability to maximize the self through the consumption of ever more goods and services. Within this view, knowledge is treated like cash to be earned and then exchanged for educational honors and eventually economic rewards. More recently, this logic has expanded and become even more explicit through both teacher bonus pay and payment to students for grades, as well as the linkage of teacher and administrator preparation to student test scores. In these examples, testing is used as if it is a neutral and objective "market" that serves—that is, a medium for the acquisition, display, and exchange of knowledge, rewarding talent and work. Of course, not only are the politics of knowledge behind the framing, selection, and organization of knowledge denied in this view, but the broader public implications of learning and the public role of schools is evacuated in favor of a metaphor of markets and consumption.

This explicit equation of educational activity with the promise of greater and greater levels of consumption is made to the nation as well as to the individual. The nation's school kids must work hard in schools to compete globally with other nations to maintain or increase our nation's consuming capacity. In this zero-sum game, the losing poorer nations end up with the role of doing the brutal labor necessary to produce the commodities in the retail stores of the richer nations. This educational promise has no way of dealing with the global race to the bottom for cheaper and cheaper labor and worsened labor conditions, nor does it deal with the structural push for cheaper and cheaper labor domestically. As some, such as Stanley Aronowitz, argue, expanded higher education enrollment becomes a way to disguise unemployment. As the U.S. economy has entered crisis with high unemployment, we find the largest venture philanthropies retooling their agendas to focus specifically on higher education preparation. In line with this, the Obama administration has on the one hand taken the positive step of expanding student loans and reforming the exploitative system of privatized high-interest student loan servicing (although in reality a far better goal would be to work for universal free higher education as exists in other industrialized nations). Yet on the other hand, the administration has introduced the "Race to the Top" program with its use of much-needed federal funds to push privatization in the form of charters. This program follows the logic of NCLB with the regressive use of federal money to reward only those who get in line with the agenda. While NCLB distributes resources to those with the capital and cultural capital to score well on tests, Race to the Top rewards those willing to loosen restrictions on charter school expansion. This amounts to an assault on teachers' unions and local school boards. What should not be missed is that the unfortunate language used for this presumes an exclusionary national competition standing starkly at odds with values of egalitarianism. But it also references the standard left accusation about the global economy that neoliberal capitalism fosters a "race to the bottom" as deregulation of controls over capital and privatization forces countries to compete for low-paying, no-benefit jobs. The name of the program is both a denial of the reality of the global race to the bottom and an admission that the highest aspiration of these market-based school reforms is the pathetic inclusion of students in this losing game. School reform for a progressively minded administration would at the very least put forward educational goals framed through the language of collective social aspirations. That is, educational projects could be initiated to make public forms of community and global improvement the basis for learning rather than continuing the Bush emphasis on individualized, narrowly defined academic achievement. Such projects could give students the language and theoretical and interpretive skills to comprehend the effects of oppressive social forces that they experience day to day and the intellectual tools to work to transform them.

In the case of both the individual and the nation, the market-based promise of the continuing neoliberal reform is driven by the idealized form of consumption; that is, luxury—luxury understood through greater and more glorious forms of commodity acquisition and consumer activity. The social cost of consumerism as the core educational promise includes not merely a crisis of meaning—the alienation of the individual from the self, from nature, and from others—but it also empties out the political and ethical possibilities of education as the only vision of social improvement becomes the individual promise of consumer commodity acquisition. The social cost is even greater in the sense that constantly increasing economic growth as the guiding force of the economy guarantees ecological devastation and vast inequalities in standards of living. Unlimited economic growth as the economic and educational goal is an utterly unsustainable ideal that will only result in the current heading toward ecological collapse, natural disaster, and human catastrophe. In the neoliberal view, there is no alternative to the present, and so the aim of education is to enforce the existing order—an order that is misrepresented as natural and inevitable rather than as being currently enacted through policy. There is a kind of double violence involved in the neoliberal educational project. On the one hand, it naturalizes the neoliberal economic uses of education, thereby naturalizing and misrepresenting as inevitable what are, in fact, human policies and priorities for profit accumulation above all else. On the other hand, neoliberal educational reform undermines the development of critical forms of education that would serve as the conditions for a public with the intellectual tools and dispositions to collectively solve public problems and move society on a different heading from the dead-end guarantee of unlimited growth. The anti-critical and anti-intellectual forms of schooling that are being fostered by neoliberal educational reform deprive citizens of the capacity to imagine and enact alternatives for the future in part because they fail to teach how to criticize and analyze the assumptions and ideologies undergirding claims to truth. The dispositions of curiosity, disciplined creativity, and investigation under attack by neoliberal educational reforms are crucial for fostering in citizens the skills of interpretation and social intervention and for imagining and also enacting alternatives to the present.

Conclusion: What Is to Be Done?

Venture philanthropy should be understood as part of an onslaught of neoliberal educational reforms, the assumptions of which ought to be seen as utterly discredited. The idealization of markets and deregulation and privatization appear to be untenable fundamental ideals as the public sector steps in to save private industry from itself, rescuing industry after industry. Venture philanthropy ought to be seen as another failed business-led reform of public schooling and should be considered in relation to the long history of business-led school reform that has largely resulted in the current educational inequalities. Public schooling needs to be revalued as a public institution with public purposes that are primarily for the fostering of public intellectual activity linked to social reconstruction and the activities of engaged public life.

The promise of educational exchange that is premised on the promise of consumer luxury is based on ecologically, politically, and economically destructive assumptions. It also fails to grasp what I call the originary pledge in educational exchange. As I contend in *The Gift of Education*, the students who pledge their lives and time to the public school system are owed material and symbolic counter pledges by the whole society. Neoliberal education and venture philanthropy presume that the educational exchange begins with the student owing the society for educational and economic opportunities and resources whether or not the society has historically and presently ponied up. Consequently, these approaches to school improvement begin by assuming that the basic problems stem not from the historical and systematized material and symbolic violence of unequal educational exchange but rather from a failure of individual discipline on the parts of the students and teachers; and they assume that the primary task is one of enforcing the official knowledge and program through various coercive measures. Instead, educational improvement ought to begin with the assumption that the school and the society owe the student an enormous debt incurred by the life and presence of the student. The counter pledge—the educational contract from the school and society—can be fulfilled materially only by accounting for the history of unequal material exchange not only in terms of educational resources but also in terms of material exchange generally. This means that schools should prepare students to engage material reality not just through the tools of mathematics and science, literacy, and social analysis. This means that part of what public schools should do as public democratic institutions is prepare students to play an active role in democratizing material relations outside of schools so that future citizens are equipped to participate in economic decisions about production and consumption that affect all citizens materially. As well, the educational contract from the school and the society can be fulfilled symbolically only by offering students the tools to analyze and interpret cultural, ideological, and linguistic formations in relation to broader economic and political forces. Public schools are obligated to prepare citizens-in-the-making for practices of interpretation and meaning-making as public individuals whose actions and signifying practices have public import.

In conjunction with activism and social movements, teachers and other cultural workers inevitably make meanings through their signifying practices. There are always political and pedagogical opportunities at play in not just teaching but all forms of communication. As the speed of communication increases through information technology, and as increasingly the economy is organized around the subjectivity-producing activities of immaterial labor, new opportunities unfold for producing new forms of subjectivity oriented toward emancipatory and egalitarian ideals, identifications, and practices. What keeps people assenting to endless war and corporate exploitation in the United States is not the barrel of a gun. What keeps people assenting is largely the ongoing pedagogical production of frameworks of interpretation, knowledge, and values constituted in schools and mass media that make oppression and exploitation commonsensical, desirable, and exciting rather than revolting. These knowledge-making sites are, however, highly contested. Democratic schools and a democratic society require the pedagogical production of joyful knowledge and dispositions of desire understood through human values of genuine freedom, equal social relations in all domains, the free exchange of knowledge, and the expansion of common goods and projects.

Educators and cultural workers, as well as students, policy makers, union organizers, and those committed to education for social justice need to work for the following:

1. To end tax breaks for foundations and erect a wall between giving and the use of money for education as part of a larger movement against business-driven educational reform. If money is given by private interests, then public control ought to be fully retained over the use of educational spending.
2. To stop the application of economism to educational reform. With the collapse of neoliberal assumptions, we should stop applying business metaphors and logic to educational thinking derived from discredited market fundamentalism. Metaphors not only of deregulation and privatization but also market-based framings of "competition and choice," "monopoly," "turnaround," and "efficiency" need to be dropped in favor of public language and assumptions that include equality, the public interest, public pedagogy, and a renewed language of educational obligation grounded in public democratic values. We might develop a notion of the educational contract that reworks the neoliberal view of educational obligation. The "measure" of educational progress ought not to be test scores but rather social progress measured by the dismantling of oppressive institutions and practices and the making of institutions and practices that provide contexts for egalitarian social relations, democratic debates, and dialogue in strong public spheres.

3. We should nationalize foundation wealth and give it to public educational authorities. Consider the case of the Bill and Melinda Gates Foundation wealth. Microsoft's private wealth was the result first of billions of dollars of public subsidy for the development of the computer industries, the Internet, and information technology. This has been a case of socialized funding and privatized profits. Once the public paid to develop the industries, the profit from the technologies was handed over to private companies. The public then subsidized super-rich individuals, giving to foundations tax breaks that essentially subsidized these private individuals to take control over educational policy steering. In essence, the public has paid to give control over public policy to elites who were already the beneficiaries of public funding for high-tech development, real estate riches, and retail fortunes. This circuit of privatization must be ended, and public control over public policy formation must be democratized.
4. We should understand that Gates and the other venture philanthropists are neither generous nor disinterested, and then take a cue from Pierre Bourdieu:

> The purely speculative and typically scholastic question of whether generosity and disinterestedness are possible should give way to the political question of the means that have to be implemented in order to create universes in which, as in gift economies, people have an interest in disinterestedness and generosity, or rather, are durably disposed to respect these universally respected forms of respect for the universal.[12]

Venture philanthropy is a bankrupt ideal in light of the collapse of the neoliberal market fundamentalism and its emphasis on markets as self-regulating and the expansion of the market model to all aspects of public life. The projects of applying business rationales to all aspects of public schooling ought to be recognized as a holdover from a speculative bubble economy and from neoliberal economic dictates and ideology. These business ideals and metaphors as applied to public schooling need to be not only dropped but also replaced with a recovered public sensibility, a universal value for the public schooling as a crucial part of a democratic public.[13]

3

Neoliberalism as Terrorism; or, State of Disaster Exceptionalism

Sophia A. McClennen

The connections between the hegemonic exercise of geopolitical power, the biopolitics of bare life and governmentality, and the free market doctrine of neoliberalism were nowhere more apparent than in the first round of presidential debates held on September 26, 2008. Barack Obama brought the biopolitics of neoliberalism into relief when he spoke about how the John McCain health care plan was based on the "notion that the market can always solve everything and that the less regulation we have, the better off we're going to be."[1] Obama's point was well taken, but what was missing was recognition of the fact that the idea that the market can solve all problems is necessarily linked to the idea that the United States can solve the problems of all other states. Both positions depend on the same internal logic, the same forms of exception, and the same exercise of sovereign power.

This is why the discussion during the debate about health care in the United States has to be read in relation to McCain's claims about U.S. foreign policy. In another moment in the debate McCain critiqued Obama's understanding of Central Asian politics: "I don't think that Senator Obama understands that there was a failed state in Pakistan when Musharraf came to power. Everybody who was around then and had been there and knew about it knew that it was a failed state." Though Pakistan was wrestling with problems—like tensions with India and serious poverty when Musharraf took power in a 1999 coup—it had a democratically elected government and was far from being what could be described as a "failed state"—that is, a country in social and economic collapse where the government no longer exercises authority. The question that must be asked, then, is how it becomes possible for a U.S. senator and presidential candidate to so glibly define Pakistan in that way. Who decides when a state has failed? Put differently, who is the "everyone" that knew that democratic Pakistan was a failed state?

Thus, when McCain defended his free-market-based economic policy or when he casually referred to democratic pre-Musharraf Pakistan as a "failed state" that "everyone knew about," he was demonstrating Carl Schmitt's notion of the sovereign who can decide the exception, who can make decisions precisely because he is sovereign, and whose rule is based on the inevitable absence of rules.[2] For Schmitt, the only rule is that of the sovereign who alone determines a state's friends or enemies, even in those cases when the enemies are the state's own inhabitants. In fact, one of the key arguments that I will make in this essay is that the contemporary neoliberal version of biopolitics requires an appreciation of how the disenfranchised within the United States are integrally linked to extra-national groups, whether these are stateless enemy combatants or entire nations, as in the case of Pakistan.

But, you might ask, what does this have to do with the current crisis in education? It has both everything and nothing to do with it. It has *everything* to do with education because, as we argue throughout this book, the advent of neoliberal policies has had a dramatic impact on our nation's schools at every level. But, as we've argued, the real boon for neoliberalism came after 9/11 when the war on terror served as a cover for the implementation of a number of neoliberal policies. Recognizing the link between neoliberalism and the war on terror, then, is essential to understanding the crises facing our schools today. It has *nothing* to do with education, because,

CHAPTER 3

as I'll argue here, scholars working in U.S. universities today have yet to fully analyze these trends in their geopolitical context. Too often criticisms of these trends have remained locally focused on what takes place within U.S. borders or have alternatively taken a global view without adequate reference to the U.S. context. So, the fact that these connections might seem hard to make is a direct consequence of the way that the new conditions under which we work in higher education have heightened the fragmentation not just of our labor, but also of our ideas. My goal in this chapter is to analyze the way that neoliberalism and terrorism have influenced our abilities to make necessary connections essential to understanding the current crisis in education. While education faces a series of crises, not the least of which is economic, my main interest here is on the way that the current educational structure has brought with it a particular worldview that makes it extremely difficult to understand the connections between state practices, the new neoliberal imperialism, ideas about how human life is valued, and geopolitical prejudices.

Prior to the events of 9/11 much U.S.-based American studies research focused on identity issues in a context of nationalism and critiques of nationalism. A great deal of work was done on issues of diversity, race, gender, and other challenges to identity. Against these trends scholars like Donald Pease and Amy Kaplan called for moving away from the ontological framework of nationalisms and alternatives to nationalism because of their over-investment in identity markers.[3] They suggest, in contrast, that it is time to reconsider more seriously the role of the state. Pease's analysis of Ground Zero and Kaplan's research on Guantanamo, for example, argue that any effort to reframe identity struggles requires attention to the violent repressive tactics of the U.S. state. Taking my cue from this line of critical work, I argue here that the next challenge for those of us interested in the relationship between national identities, political possibilities, and global power networks concerns understanding the practices, pedagogies, and public image of the state post 9/11.

Suggesting this line of work, though, for U.S. academics requires further attending to the troubled context for engaging in lines of inquiry that challenge the pervasive turn away from more politically incisive critique that has followed in the wake of 9/11. Arguably the turn to identity-based critique where scholars examine identity markers as the source for problems of disenfranchisement as opposed to examining political and economic structures—like capital, class, and the state—has its origins well before 9/11. One could suggest that such shifts were a function of the sorts of lines of inquiry that emerged in the 1970s and 1980s that derived from deconstruction's emphasis on negative critique and its distrust of organizing concepts in combination with poststructuralism's focus on language and signs as sources of power. Even though these critical trends developed in response to an urge to challenge oppressive power structures, when they merged with a suspicion of any efforts to find a common ground or collective good, they often resulted in positions that were wary of proffering alternatives. As Masao Miyoshi notes in his critique of the development of U.S. humanities-based research, U.S. scholars share "an undeniable common proclivity . . . to fundamentally reject such totalizing concepts as humanity, civilization, history, and justice, and such subtotalities as a region, a nation, a locality, or even any smallest group."[4] This emphasis on difference without an external referent ultimately strips criticism of its context and makes any analysis of state structures difficult to sustain.

These trends then combined with the self-censorship and weak, if not totally bland, forms of critical engagement that followed from the academic witch hunts launched by the post-9/11 assaults on higher education.[5] As Henry Giroux notes in *The University in Chains*, the post-9/11 assaults on higher education by various right-wing constituencies were met all too often by apathy on the part of progressive academics, who were either too afraid or too overwhelmed to offer any sort of sustained resistance. According to Giroux, "given the seriousness of the current attack on higher education by an alliance of diverse right-wing forces, it is difficult to understand why the majority of liberals, progressives, and left-oriented educators has become relatively silent or tacit apologists in the face of the assault."[6] Moreover, as evidenced by Stanley Fish's interventions in *The Chronicle of Higher Education* in pieces like "Aim Low" and "Save the World on Your Own Time," the post-9/11 combination of terror and neoliberal practices led to an "officialspeak" by many academics in positions of power that effectively shut down a number of critical avenues of scholarly work and civic engagement. In his article "Save the World on Your Own Time," Fish states unequivocally: "my assertion is that it is immoral for academics or for academic institutions to proclaim moral views."[7] From Fish's viewpoint, focusing on skills and disciplinary competence is the central mission of higher education, and teaching moral and civic responsibility is not only a bad idea, it is unworkable.[8] Fish's claims would have likely been divisive regardless of the context within which they appeared, but it is fair to say that their publication in the midst of debates about the morality of the war in Iraq, the curtailing of civil rights post 9/11 in the United States, and the chilling atmosphere on university campuses caused by the USA PATRIOT Act and other legislation served to exacerbate the ongoing debates about the role of politics, social critique, and intellectual engagement in classrooms.

But the problems go even deeper than the post-9/11 climate of censorship and self-censorship, since, as I argue in "Neoliberalism and the Crisis of Intellectual Engagement," faculty working in neoliberally inclined universities find themselves with less and less time to dedicate to serious reflection.[9] Every year brings higher expectations for publishing, for teaching more students, for serving on more committees, and so on, while academic jobs have become more and more precarious. Add to that the major funding cuts for research on global issues as described in the introduction and we can begin to see the range of factors that have made work on the geopolitics of terror-based, neoliberal imperialism difficult to sustain and advance. When we combine the material effects of the way that the work of higher education has been shifting with the practices and ideologies of neoliberalism and the war on terror, we can begin to see the depth of this crisis. In this context, then, it comes as little surprise that there has been relatively little attention paid to the way that 9/11 facilitated a shift in state power, where democratic institutions entered into a permanent state of exception and citizens were indefinitely denied their rights. But, as I will argue here, attention to the connections between neoliberalism's need to push the state to defend the rights of the market over the rights of the citizen and the war on terror's restructuring of rights both within the United States and across nations is a much-needed if not essential line of work for any scholar committed to restoring the democratic possibilities of higher education. One of the greatest threats to progressive education in the United States today comes from the blind acceptance of corporate mentalities, the incorporation of militaristic solutions to conflict, and the demonization of other cultures, all of which combine to further a state of *terror education*.

One issue that is often overlooked is that the war on terror's merger with the corporate state of neoliberalism has radically altered civic identities on U.S. soil and abroad. In one example, the shared criminalization of the immigrant, the refugee, and the disaster victim points to new ways that identities have been reconfigured as hostile to "freedom," where "freedom" refers to the sovereign free market rather than to individual rights. We might think of Lou Dobbs's vicious attacks on undocumented U.S. labor coupled with Fox News reports on the war. After mapping the theoretical implications of linking neoliberalism with biopolitical practices of the war on terror's suspension of civil rights, the first part of this essay traces this new U.S. state, what I am describing as "The Neoliberal State of Disaster Exceptionalism." I then examine this transformation in the particular context of U.S.-Afghan relations, where I analyze the dialectics between sovereign states and what I call *bare states*, that is, states that are included in the geopolitical world system by virtue of their exclusion. Unlike the war in Iraq, the war in Afghanistan has from the outset been described as an effort to rescue a failed state from terrorist influences. Any disasters caused by the U.S. invasion are always justified by the previously existing Afghan state of disaster. Reading both mainstream media accounts of the U.S. attacks on Afghanistan post 9/11 and fictional efforts to narrate Afghanistan (particularly the novel *The Kite Runner* and the film *Charlie Wilson's War*), I argue that the representation of Afghanistan and of U.S.-Afghan relations both reveals and conceals the intersections between neoliberalism, terrorism, and the state of exception.

The Neoliberal State of Disaster Exceptionalism

Much of my argument rests on the idea that the post-9/11 state requires attention to a new biopolitical era—one that links the state of exception with the free market state of neoliberalism. Although a number of scholars have taken up post-9/11 biopolitics and a number of others have focused on the effects of neoliberalism, few have claimed that these two structuring systems are necessarily linked. Naomi Klein brings some of these threads together in her study of disaster capitalism, arguing that neoliberalism thrives on disaster and shock to radically alter civic structures and state roles.[10] Henry Giroux and Zygmunt Bauman have also claimed that neoliberalism brings with it a specific set of biopolitical practices that radically alter the notion of the citizen and the public sphere.[11] What these scholars have shown is that there is a symbiotic convergence between neoliberal free market capitalism, which understands citizens as consumers or as disposable waste, and an emergency state, which increasingly abrogates the rights of entire populations in the name of homeland security. Regardless of whether the punishing force is the market or the permanent state of war, the result is an onslaught on rights, both civic and corporal.

These new identity formations created by the post-9/11 U.S. state, though, also rely on earlier paradigms, most significantly that of U.S. exceptionalism and that of bare life. American exceptionalism depends on the long-standing belief that the United States differs qualitatively from other developed nations—a difference that makes it possible, for instance, for the United States to be critical of British or Russian/Soviet imperialism but not of its own. That the United States is superior to developing or undeveloped nations is taken for granted. Thus the bombing of civilians in Iraq or Afghanistan is justified whereas the terrorist bombings of U.S. civilians are not. What is of particular interest in the current context is the link between U.S. exceptionalism and bare life. Giorgio Agamben's theory of bare life claims that state power has always assumed power over life, deciding who will receive the rights of the citizen and who will not.[12] Bare life is that life which is included in the state by virtue of its exclusion from political life. It is life that can be killed with impunity because it is a life without rights. Agamben points out that "if anything characterizes modern democracy over classical democracy . . . it is that modern democracy presents itself from the beginning as a vindication and liberation of [bare life]."[13] But the rights of the citizen in the modern state still face two problems: first, sovereign power creates bare life even in modernity, and, second, the increasing commonality of the state of exception, or the suspension of law in order to establish rule, makes it possible for all citizens to be immediately rendered as bare life and to be stripped of their rights.

According to Agamben, the United States entered a state of exception shortly after the 9/11 terrorist attacks when it enacted a series of laws that governed living beings by means of the suspension of law. But this retraction of rights was read in keeping with U.S. exceptionalism as fundamentally different from the suspension of rights as practiced by other states. So, a key feature that affects how we think of this problem is the way that the United States' dominant narrative as a free, democratic nation that is globally exceptional frustrates

CHAPTER 3

any counter claims that suggest that, in contrast, the United States is like all other states that have limited citizens' rights as a means of preserving power. Pease analyzes these trends in *The New American Exceptionalism* by asking why citizens would willingly cede their rights in order to protect an idea of American exceptionalism that became progressively distant from their experience of everyday life. He explains this development as a psychosocial process whereby the citizen fantasizes an active role in the suspension of rule such that they imagine themselves as agents of rather than victims of the national security state. "Rather than protesting against the state's abrogation of its rules, U.S. citizens fantasized themselves as the sovereign power that had suspended law in the name of securing the nation."[14] By making the case of the United States' suspension of rights incomparable, and therefore exceptional, the dominant narrative of U.S. power is then able to suggest that the United States remains in a unique position, as a consequence of its exceptional democracy, to determine the fate of other states.

If U.S. exceptionalism is a geopolitical policy and bare life refers to the rights of the being within the borders of a particular state, what happens when these spheres can no longer be kept separate? When what a state does within its borders necessarily leaks to the global sphere and vice versa? As a way of interrogating the geopolitical implications of these mutual contaminations it is first necessary to consider the global implications and ideologies that derive from Agamben's theories of the state of exception and bare life. Considered thusly, it becomes clear that the U.S. state of exception requires American exceptionalism and depends not just on bare life but also on *bare states*, that is, on the designation of states that are included in the world order solely by the form of their exclusion. In addition to rethinking the false binary of internal and external state policies, a further part of my argument is that it is essential to recognize the symbiosis between free market capitalism and the perpetual state of exception.

Agamben's focus on the force of law misses an opportunity to elaborate on the force of capital—a word that never appears, for instance, in his *State of Exception*.[15] Unchecked free market capitalism requires the state of exception because the deregulation of the market necessitates the destruction of the public sphere and the permanent suspension of the rights of the citizen. As mentioned earlier these ideas are latently developed in Klein's theory of disaster capitalism. Klein argues that the blank slate caused by disaster allows for massive transformations in state policy. She links megadisasters—wars, massive recessions, and natural disasters—with superprofits. The disaster is the event that sanctions an abrupt shift in the function of the state, one that always brings with it a loss of rights because the state protects capital rather than people, at the same time that it signals an opportunity for neoliberal practices. A further key component of Klein's theories of neoliberalism is her attention to the biopolitics of shock, where shock affects not just markets but bodies, a move that allows her to link torture and a pervasive culture of fear with the functioning of the free market. She makes a comparison among the United States' research into psychological military operations, torture tactics, and the fostering of mass hysteria after major disasters and argues that these biopolitical practices pave the way for societies to willingly cede rights and dignity in favor of so-called security and stability. What Klein's theory lacks, though, is more attention to the ideological forces that make these shifts possible, especially the history of U.S. exceptionalism, in addition to orientalism and its sister stereotypes. Moreover, just as Agamben misses capitalism as a biopolitical force, Klein misses the biopolitics of governmentality. My claim is that the current forms of state power require that we put these theories into dialogue.

The theorist who has most worked on establishing these links is Henry Giroux, who considers neoliberalism a form of public pedagogy—a hegemonic force that teaches the public to accept unacceptable social practices. Giroux, along with the late Pierre Bourdieu, has been one of the foremost theorists of the ideology and public pedagogy of neoliberal practices. As Giroux explains it, "What is often ignored by theorists who analyze the rise of neoliberalism in the United States is that it is not only a system of economic power relations but also a political project, intent on producing new forms of subjectivity and sanctioning particular modes of conduct."[16] In recent years, a number of theorists (e.g., Agamben, Hardt, Negri, and Mbembe) have also begun to expand on Michel Foucault's theory of biopolitics—the theory of how states govern via the regulation of human life. But Giroux is one of the few scholars to develop a theory of neoliberal biopolitics and of how these practices have been directly influenced by the post-9/11 militarization of the U.S. security state. The book that most explores these links is *Against the Terror of Neoliberalism*. There Giroux writes, "[Neoliberalism's] supporting political culture and pedagogical practices also put into play a social universe and cultural landscape that sustain a particularly barbaric notion of authoritarianism, set in motion under the combined power of a religious and market fundamentalism and anti-terrorism laws that suspend civil liberties, incarcerate disposable populations, and provide the security forces necessary for capital to destroy those spaces where democracy can be nourished."[17] For Giroux "Democratic politics is increasingly depoliticized by the intersection of a free-market fundamentalism and an escalating militarism" that not only attacks civil liberties within the United States but also designates entire populations outside of the United States as either disposable or controllable.[18]

Afghanistan as a Bare State

U.S.-Afghan relations post 9/11 offer a tragic, yet paradigmatic, example of this new biopolitical era. Unlike the war in Iraq, the war in Afghanistan has from the outset been described as an effort to rescue a failed state. While much time has been spent, especially on the part of Noam Chomsky and Jacques

Derrida, deconstructing the definitions and tracing the auto-referentiality of terms like "failed states" and "rogue states," it seems to me that the more relevant way of thinking about these issues is through the dialectic of what I call the *bare state* and the sovereign state. If the sovereign has the ability to decide which lives can be killed due to the suspension of the force of law, then it follows that the sovereign *state*, that is the state that rules all other states, decides which states will be bare states. The sovereign state imposes the rules that determine the exception. Bare states are those that can be destroyed or manipulated with impunity because they are only included in the world system by their exclusion, by the assumption that they have no rights to self-govern. The destruction of the bare state by the sovereign state has no legal ramifications because the bare state has no rights. The focus on the developed world in the theories of Schmitt and then also in Agamben ignores the problem of states where the sovereignty of the sovereign is always in question. In a sense imperialism is the state of exception *writ large*, and when states do emerge as a consequence of postcolonial independence, that independence is akin to *bare* independence: it is an independence that exists only at the discretion of the sovereign state.

Afghanistan is a particularly complex case because it is best described as a quasi-postcolonial state. Although it has resisted foreign rule, it has had plenty of foreign interference. Located at a geographical crossroads, it is a state that came into existence in order to resist the imperial designs of the British and Russian Great Game in the nineteenth and twentieth centuries. And, as is commonly the case with postcolonial states, the Afghan state was carved across ethnic lines and according to imperially imposed geographic boundaries. The key issue, however, is that states like Afghanistan are encouraged by sovereign states to operate in ways that undermine the rights of their citizens so as to justify their continued exclusion from geopolitical state rights. As Rudyard Kipling puts it in his story of Afghanistan, "The Man Who Would Be King," "nobody cares a straw for the internal administration of Native States so long as oppression and crime are kept within decent limits, and the ruler is not drugged, drunk, or diseased from one end of the year to another. They are the dark places of the earth, full of unimaginable cruelty."[19] Here orientalism combines with the idea of the bare state. Not only is it assumed that this is a state that needs oversight and that this is a state where citizens will have few rights if any, but it is also assumed that the so-called sovereign of the bare state is genetically incapable of just rule.

The problem for bare states in the era of neoliberalism is not only their lack of rights within the world system but also the fact that the deregulative ideologies that buttress the sovereign state/bare state dialectic are linked to the needs of market fundamentalism. Arguably neoliberalism is simply the most recent phase of capitalism, the one that most visibly exposes the rule of the market as the only rule that capitalism will recognize. The deregulation required by neoliberals is closely linked to the lack of rights of bare life. Under neoliberalism people are products and states protect the rights of corporations rather than of citizens. Thus when neoliberalism joins the imperialist bare state/sovereign state structure the result is that the only rules are that there are no rules except those articulated by the sovereign system of capital. Of course in the case of Afghanistan the idea that the area and its inhabitants represented nothing more than products to be exchanged or bodies to be regulated had a long history that predated the United States' involvement there.

These ideas of a barbaric land occupied by barbaric people would re-emerge with particular force in representations of Afghanistan after 9/11.[20] Much was heard of the brutality of Taliban rule, of the plight of Afghan women, and of the tenacious spirit of the Afghan warrior who had managed to defend his country from foreign rule for more than 2,000 years. The most frequently cited resource was that of Rudyard Kipling, and Corinne Fowler writes that "during the 2001 conflict, references to Kipling were legion."[21] For instance, while in Peshawar at the American club, British journalist Ben Macintyre wrote that the spies, arms dealers, aid workers, mercenaries, and journalists that congregated there all had one thing in common: they all read Kipling as they lived out their "romantic fantasies." "The works of Rudyard Kipling were required reading, for Britain's bard of imperialism captured the wilderness and the wonder of the North-West Frontier like no other writer, before or since."[22] Kipling's works were cited throughout media reports in the days following 9/11 as though they provided some deep insight into the mystery of Afghanistan and its neighboring countries. News reports carried multiple references from his short story "The Man Who Would Be King" and from his poem "The Young British Soldier," which portrays Afghans (including women) as particularly brutal:

> When you're wounded and left on Afghanistan's plains,
> And the women come out to cut up what remains,
> Jest roll to your rifle and blow out your brains
> An' go to your Gawd like a soldier.[23]

The turn to Kipling may very well have made sense as the United States and Britain contemplated overt military action in a country with a reputation for rebelling against superior military force. Not only had the Brits suffered military losses there three times (1842, 1841, and 1919), but the Soviet conflict in Afghanistan from 1979 to 1989 arguably led to the end of the Soviet Union. Perhaps some of Kipling's insights into these conflicts could serve as useful cautions. Nevertheless, the repeated use of Kipling as a source of knowledge about Afghanistan points to the persistence of *orientalism* in the post-9/11 context.

Edward Said suggests that one of the key features of orientalist thinking is the assumed fact that there is a fundamental distinction between "Orient" and "Occident." But this distinction is not one of simple difference; it is one of hierarchy. This strategy means that, regardless of the relationship between west and east, the west always retains *"positional* superiority."[24] This positional superiority holds material force when we link this idea to the concept of the sovereign state that determines the fate of the bare state, bringing with it a global biopolitics that not only separates categories of humanity within nations but across them as well. Thus, when U.S. Navy Seal Marc Luttrell describes his mission to Afghanistan as "payback time for the World Trade Center," he is a "special breed of warrior" whereas his enemy is described as "lawless," "wild mountain men."[25] Or when Afghans rebel against foreign invasion, they are described as dangerous and unpredictable, but when western countries defend themselves from foreign invasion, they are described as righteous and valiant. Not only does such thinking depend on an absolute division between east and west, where the west is always understood as superior to the east, but it also requires that east and west be understood as static entities that do not significantly change over time and that do not have substantial variations within themselves. Such practices meant that it remained possible after 9/11 to assume that Kipling's imperialist view of the barbarous nature of Afghanistan was still largely true, that little had changed, and they depended on ignoring Kipling's own context of writing as one that referred to a specific historical moment that carried particular worldviews. The third key feature of orientalism relevant for a discussion of the bare state is that it depends on ideas and not simply on the use of military and political power to remain in force. When orientalist statements are made in the western media about Afghanistan, such statements themselves serve to strengthen structures of authority that are not only material but also hegemonic. Thus, Kipling's legacy was continued in western media representations of Operation Enduring Freedom not simply through references to his works, but also through the mere practice of producing truth claims about Afghanistan, the nature of the Afghan people, and their relationship to the west—truth claims that inevitably reinforced the historical legacy of occident versus orient.

For obvious reasons post-9/11 U.S. media coverage did not replicate the British media's imperialist anxieties, but that did not deter U.S. journalists from falling into a pattern of repeatedly rehearsing a series of traits that indelibly marked Afghanistan as a threat to western ways of life. Mahmood Mamdani refers to these practices as "culture talk." Building on Edward Said's concept of *orientalism*, contemporary culture talk takes its cues from works like Samuel Huntington's *Clash of Civilizations* and understands contemporary conflicts in cultural rather than political terms. Mamdani explains that "It is no longer the market (capitalism), nor the state (democracy), but culture (modernity) that is said to be the dividing line between those in favor of a peaceful, civic existence and those inclined to terror."[26] The key to culture talk is the assumption that different cultures have different essences, and it requires that cultures be understood outside of their historical and political context. In the west post-9/11 culture talk meant understanding the crisis in Afghanistan as one that was culturally endemic, that of a failure to become civilized, rather than as a consequence of specific historical and political developments. As a result, post-9/11 Afghan-related reporting often included references to the rise of fundamentalist Islam in the country but rarely acknowledged the role played in Afghanistan by Saudi Arabia's and Pakistan's intelligence agencies (the GID and ISI), who worked during the Soviet era along with the CIA to help train and fund the Afghan rebels who would later become the Taliban.

Instead of contextually and historically specific reporting, much news relied on a series of orientalist, culturalist stereotypes of Afghanistan that reinforced a biopolitics of Afghan disposability. One ongoing and persistent feature of media coverage referred to the warlike nature of Afghans and to the fact that Afghans "have traditionally greeted outside armies with hostility."[27] Fowler also notes that "a striking feature of news media coverage of the 2001 bombing campaign" depicted Afghanistan as "contemporaneous with medieval Europe"—a condition that suggested the almost total lack of anything the west would call "civilization" in the nation.[28] Another trope of the media was the reference to the lack of national unity in a country prone to tribalism and ethnic conflict. Ross Benson writes, for instance, that "each ethnic group is distrustful of the other and in Afghanistan distrust is cause enough for murder."[29] Linked to descriptions of the people as barbarous, uncivilized, premodern and dangerous, the physical geography was described as equally treacherous, sometimes due to the ominous mountains and deserts and sometimes due to the wreckage left behind, remnants of the Soviet era.[30] All of these practices combine, then, to offer a cultural logic to treating Afghanistan as a bare state and to characterize Afghans as undeserving of self-determination.

As a counterforce to much mass media reporting of the conflict, a series of cultural texts attempted to offer an alternative view. Bringing public attention to another side of the story was one of the motives behind Mike Nichols's film *Charlie Wilson's War*—a quasi-farce about the United States' role in exacerbating conflict during the Soviet Union's occupation of Afghanistan from 1979 to 1989 that was produced by Participant Productions, a company dedicated to "entertainment that inspires and compels social change."[31] While Nichols does not do enough to link the so-called "freedom fighters" of the Soviet conflict with the "barbaric" mujahideen of the post-9/11 moment, the strength of his film is its narrative of U.S. exceptionalism's use of Afghanistan as a bare state. The film traces the unlikely story of Charlie Wilson, a playboy Texas Congressman, who singlehandedly raised the budget for the covert operations in Afghanistan from 35 million dollars in 1982 to 600 million in 1987. Wilson's interest in Afghanistan stems from the twin desires to "kill Russians" and to help the Afghans, whom he meets for the first time in a devastating scene in a Pakistani refugee camp. The film does an excellent job of pointing out the contradictions of U.S. exceptionalism that link humanitarian aid with a devastating proxy war. Nichols also underscores the idea of Afghanistan as a bare state when he has a CIA member refer to it as "barely a country"—a move that links a state with no rights in the global system to a state that lacks the infrastructure of modernity. One example of this combined bareness is a scene where characters complain about how Afghanistan's lack of roads makes it less convenient for them to provide anti-Soviet forces with weapons.

Telling this story in the context of the United States' ongoing overt war with Afghanistan, where thousands of Afghan civilians have died, where Afghans constitute the largest refugee population worldwide, and where only 6 percent of the country even had intermittent electricity in 2004, goes a long way to correcting the myths and misinformation about the state of Afghanistan.[32] But the film also has a few blind spots, not the least of which is the lack of voice given to Afghans themselves, who are almost always screened from a distance, often in scenes that show them being gunned down by Soviets, a practice that tends to justify the role of the United States in the covert war by reinforcing orientalist stereotypes of Afghans as incomprehensible others who needed to be rescued by the United States.

In contrast to *Charlie Wilson's War*, putting a human face on Afghans was one of the primary goals of Khaled Hosseini's enormously successful *The Kite Runner* (2003).[33] The narrative covers the life of a boy who grows up in Afghanistan prior to the Soviet invasion, takes refuge in Pakistan and then later the United States, only to later return to Taliban-led Afghanistan on a quest for personal redemption. Most post-9/11 writing by Afghans falls into the category of "burqa lit" and, even though a number of these books, such as *My Forbidden Face* and *Zoya's Story*, were written by women who lived in moderate Islamic homes with men who did not abuse them, these books tended to focus wholly on the brutality of Taliban rule, which often reinforced a view of Afghan barbarity.[34] Hosseini's text, in contrast, portrays Kabul before the Soviet invasion in significant detail giving western readers a view of a moment in Afghan history when the city was "modern" and "civilized" by western standards. Even though the novel takes a highly romantic and nostalgic tone, a stylistic feature that may be explained by Hosseini's status as an exile from his homeland, these lyrical portraits of the city challenged assumptions that Afghanistan had been always a barbaric and medieval nation with no connection to modernity.

This is the novel's greatest strength, but it is largely eclipsed by its weaknesses, which include reducing the existence of the Taliban regime to the moral failure of its protagonist and the psychological flaws of his nemesis, Assef, the Taliban thug who is simply described as a sociopath. Unfortunately, though, the balance between Afghan specificity and "universal" (read western) themes has been largely lost on western readers. Meghan O'Rourke notes that most readers overlooked or downplayed those features of the novel that indicated "otherness": "Study the 631 Amazon reviews and scores of newspaper features about *The Kite Runner*, and you'll find that most fail to mention that the narrator converts from a secular Muslim to a devoutly practicing one. Hosseini's story indulges this readerly impulse to downplay what is hard to grasp and play up what seems familiar."[35] The fact that the novel did not seem foreign was precisely one of Hosseini's goals. In an interview he explained that "It goes back to telling a story that connects with people on a human level. When you do that, I think you get people thinking."[36] The dilemma, though, is that in order for *The Kite Runner* to depict Afghans as humans, as part of a universal, global community, they almost lost their Afghanness.

Conveniently, the novel's presentation of Afghanistan's problems ignores global geopolitics and the history of U.S. manipulation. At a moment when U.S. citizens had to grapple with terrorist attacks on U.S. soil, such a tale suggested a division between good and evil that inevitably palliated the violent consequences of bombing Afghanistan and that made it easier to imagine that the invasion was a just response. Even though *Charlie Wilson's War* and *The Kite Runner* were both interested in correcting western misinformation about Afghanistan, by dealing with pre-9/11 Afghanistan they risk leaving audiences ambivalent about whether or not the post-9/11 U.S. invasion was a justified humanitarian action.

The story most ignored is the one of how the U.S. invasion has brought a neoliberal spin to the Afghan bare state. As a corrective, Ann Jones's journalistic memoir *Kabul in Winter* explains the new neoliberal economics of aid and military action at work in Afghanistan post 9/11.[37] Aid, like war, is outsourced, allowing contractors to gain lucrative deals that re-funnel U.S. funds back to the private sector. She explains that because "the underlying purpose of American aid is to make the world safe and open to American business, business is cut in from the start."[38] And to prove the point that U.S. policies have rendered Afghans as bare life without rights and without the ability to participate in the market, Afghan contractors are excluded from competing for these deals because, as one USAID official puts it, "they don't know [U.S.] methods of accounting."[39]

As I close this necessarily sketchy outline of the links between neoliberalism, the state of exception, and a new era of biopolitical practices what remains clear is that the productive tensions over the public sphere and over enlightenment commitments to rights and just wars that had existed prior to the rise of neoliberalism have been almost entirely dismantled. Market fundamentalism and corporate rights have become the rule that determines law with none, or virtually none, of the push back of humanistic, egalitarian, and democratic ideals. As complex and contradictory as those ideals may have been, their absence under the neoliberal state of exception makes possible entirely new forms of human devastation and states of terror. Understanding the new era of the neoliberal state of disaster exceptionalism requires attention not just to changes in state policies, rights, and biopolitical practices, but also to the ideologies and counter-narratives that support and resist them.

As I come full circle to the ways that these issues intersect with the current crisis in education, my goal is to suggest that one of the most pernicious consequences of these shifts has been their influence on faculty research and teaching. For the past four years I have taught about Afghanistan in my human rights course and I have been consistently surprised by how few students can even name the countries that border Afghanistan, let alone recount the series of steps that led the United States to decide to go to war there. Surely the lack of interest and knowledge about a nation where we are at war is evidence of a U.S. attitude toward Afghanistan that conceives of it as a bare state. Similarly there has been a surprising lack of scholarship on the topic from the ranks of humanists who arguably are well-equipped to read the intersections of ideologies, political practices, and forms of cultural expression. The reasons for this lack, as explained in the introduction to this book, relate not only to campus practices and faculty interests, but also to the ways in which government support for funding research and teaching on global issues has brought with it an atmosphere of surveillance and a disinterest in encouraging faculty to be experts on certain topics that are arguably of extreme national interest. I don't mean to sidestep the other major areas in which neoliberalism and terrorism have combined to affect higher education, but I do want to suggest that one of the major areas that deserves our attention is precisely in how we teach and lecture and write about the new state structures that have emerged in the era of neoliberal imperialism. Attending to the links between neoliberalism, post-9/11 U.S. imperialism, and the new biopolitical configurations these developments have caused is our next challenge.

4

On Academic Terrorism

Neoliberalism, Higher Education, and the Politics of Emotion

Jeffrey R. Di Leo

Higher education in America is undergoing some radical changes. Many within the academy fear that they are changes for the worse—and that the vision of the academy they believe in is on the brink of complete destruction. Whereas twentieth-century American professors enjoyed a high degree of control over university curricula and the fundamental right to critically inquire into any subject without fear of losing their position within the university, academics in the new millennium are facing increasing degrees of curricular scrutiny, as well as department closures, unreasonable expectations, and job insecurity. This coupled with the possibility of academic life without tenure or academic freedom has fundamentally affected their emotional response to academe.

One of the major causes of these changes in the academy is the escalating trend to see higher education as a type of business or corporation. In the business world, products are marketed and produced with the aim of growing market

CHAPTER 4

share, and values and processes are determined by their ability to raise sales and profitability. The application of increasingly severe versions of this operational philosophy to the academy has in large part contributed to the move toward contingent faculty appointments, a vocationally based curriculum, and the curtailing of critical freedoms. If this situation is not reversed, there is a strong possibility that the university of the future will be more like a vocational training center staffed by part-time instructors than a nexus of critical inquiry facilitated by full-time professors.

It is within these conditions, namely, the well-documented rise of the corporate university—and the fall of university culture as we have known it—that I would like to briefly consider the politics of emotion in academe. Although a relatively neglected area of metaprofessional and educational inquiry, the emotional world created within higher education is an important aspect of academic life.[1] Students pursuing their studies with a preponderance of joy and a feeling of optimism are preferable to those pursuing them with fear and a feeling of nervousness.[2] Much the same holds true for the faculty who teach them and the administrators who facilitate relations among students and faculty. Faculty conducting teaching, scholarship, and service with joy and feelings of pride and optimism are becoming more difficult to find, and administrators relaying fearful messages and projecting nervousness and apprehension about academe's future are in no short supply. I point this out because I believe that higher education in America has taken an emotional turn for the worse in the new millennium, particularly after the attacks of September 11, 2001—and this is having a debilitating effect on efforts to confront the consequences of the corporate university and educational neoliberalism. In the remainder of this chapter, I'd like to propose that the primary emotional effect of neoliberalism in education is *fear*, and that the promotion of neoliberal academic policies is itself a type of terrorism, namely, *academic* terrorism.

The Last Corporate University

The economic and political dimensions of universities have become a very hot and contested topic of late—especially within scholarly organizations affiliated with the humanities. It is not uncommon now to find, for example, standing room audiences at the Modern Language Association (MLA) or American Comparative Literature Association (ACLA) for presentations about the job market or the fate of tenure, while sessions devoted to subjects such as comparative arts or Chaucer have more empty seats than full ones. Indeed, one of the major contributions of the rise of cultural studies in our profession is the normalization of metaprofessional scholarship, particularly among committed humanities professors. Although the profession of literary studies has by far been the loudest and most articulate voice in this discussion (bolstered in part by Cary Nelson, an English professor, who recently served as president of the American Association of University Professors), other humanities disciplines such as philosophy and history have not been far behind.[3]

What is important to recall is that prior to the rise of cultural studies in the late 1980s and 1990s, discussion of the metaprofessional dimensions of the university were nowhere as dominant as they are today. Philosophy professors used to research and write about philosophy, and English professors about literature. These were the hot topics at scholarly meetings, while metaprofessional subjects such as the job market, academic publishing, and tenure were primarily discussed in the lounge over coffee. Although students and professors definitely had strong opinions on these subjects and shared many of the same concerns that are in vogue today about the job market, salaries, job security, and publishing, they were not things that were widely regarded as fair game for conference presentation, let alone scholarly publication.

We've come a long way though over the past twenty years. The publication of books like Bruce Wilshire's *The Moral*

CHAPTER 4

Collapse of the University: Professionalism, Purity, and Alienation (1990), Stanley Fish's *Professional Correctness: Literary Studies and Political Change* (1995), and David Damrosch's *We Scholars: Changing the Culture of the University* (1995) opened the door for taking these discussions out of the coffee lounge and into the scholarly forum. If major scholars in our field, for example, Wilshire in philosophy, Fish in English, and Damrosch in comparative literature, were publishing scholarly works on the economic and political life of the academy, then the rest of us could—and should—too. The book, however, that kicked the door down—and radically altered the nature of metaprofessional discourse—was one by a relatively unknown associate professor of comparative literature at the Université de Montréal.

Bill Reading's *The University in Ruins*, which was published in 1996, turned the humanists' discussion of the academy decidedly more political and economic. And his book, more than any other from this period, established the role of the market in the administration of universities as a central topos in our metaprofessional deliberations. Soon the phrase "corporate university" came to be the central signifier for everything that is wrong with universities in America. Excellent books such as Derek Bok's *Universities in the Marketplace* (2003) and David Kirp's *Shakespeare, Einstein, and the Bottom Line* (2003) continued to hammer home this point over the next fifteen years. These and other studies inform us that universities in America have been and continue to be run more like businesses or corporations than, well, universities.[4]

However, in spite of their collective insights on the corporatization of the university, considerations of the general emotional state of the academy under these conditions are largely ignored. Moreover, the majority of the studies published in the past ten years continue this trend. In addition (and somewhat surprisingly), most recent studies of university conditions do not even discuss the attacks of September 11, 2001, or the repressive, neoliberal educational policies established in the wake of these events, both of which play a large role in the contemporary emotional condition of academe. A good example is the much-discussed and very popular recent study by an Ohio State University English professor.

In *The Last Professors: The Corporate University and the Fate of the University* (2008), Frank Donoghue predicts that while "professors have only been around for the last eighty years,"[5] don't count on them being around for the next eighty. In the process, he makes no pretense about having a solution to this situation, and clearly states, "I offer nothing in the way of uplifting solutions to the problems that I describe."[6] Rather, Donoghue simply aims to show both how we got into this situation, and why we are not going to be able to get out of it. The emotional condition of faculty caught in this downward spiral is not his concern.

Although his honesty about this is commendable, the fact that he does not propose any solutions begs the question as to the purpose of the book, particularly when so much had already been written about this subject. The bibliography to Donoghue's book has almost two hundred entries, most of which confirm his point that corporate logic and values provided the foundational and continuing conditions of the university in America. While it is interesting to read, for example, about the ways in which business interests have historically tempered and contained the humanities, it is disappointing to find not even a glimmer of a *defense* of the humanities against corporate interests or an attempt to help emotionally affected faculty resolve this situation. What does one say, for example, to a business person, university regent, or a state legislator who asks why *should* we support the humanities in higher education rather than "to provide students with skills to succeed in business"? What does one say to an emotionally distraught colleague whose work in the humanities is deemed unimportant or inessential? Studies without such insight are of limited value in times of well-known academic crisis.

Moreover, and perhaps more problematic, is the lack of effort to argue that corporate values such as efficiency, productivity, and usefulness are in themselves the wrong values for the academy (even though Donoghue finds them to be "oppressive"[7]). Statements like "the very corporate values from which we humanists wish to distance ourselves"[8] pepper the book, although it is never demonstrated that values such as "usefulness" are ones from which *we humanists* need to distance ourselves—after all, isn't, for example, usefulness the cornerstone of American pragmatism, which is itself a paradigmatic example of American humanism?

As such, Donoghue's book is not a defense of the values that the academy should have, and not an argument against the values that it does have. Nor does it make any effort to contend with the devastating emotional effect of negatively received academic values on faculty. In this respect, Donoghue's book is not that different from most of the other recent studies of the corporate university: lots of description of problems with faculty salaries, tenure, adjunct hiring, loss of research support, decrease in publishing opportunities, and so on, but with little insight on how to get out of this situation or how to emotionally cope with it.[9]

Unfortunately, studies like Donoghue's are far too common. Although their doom-and-gloom snapshots of academe may make for good summer reading, they must be regarded as missed opportunities to work toward a revaluation of the academy—and the demise of the corporate university. Instead of simply bemoaning long-standing oppressive values underlying academic culture, scholars like Donoghue need to use the negative emotional response these values elicit from students, faculty, and administrators to build a case for their revaluation. Instead of repeating shopworn assessments of the problems facing higher education, we need to use the unpleasant intensification of fear and terror in higher education—brought about by neoliberal responses to the attacks of September 11, 2001—to bring about the twilight of the corporate university. Studies of the university that offer no speculative position out of the neoliberal abyss only promote academic fear and terror, which is itself the primary fuel of educational neoliberalism.

Death of the Neoliberal Arts

Since 9/11, not only has military funding of university research increased, but support has risen for academic programs that encourage the militarization of higher education.[10] But at what cost? During this same period, funding for humanities scholarship and research aimed at fundamental social and environmental issues has decreased, and liberal arts coursework and programs have been cut back. In this context, the liberal arts and critical studies in American higher education are better labeled the *neo*liberal arts and *un*critical studies. What is even worse is the way in which neoliberal ways of viewing higher education and the liberal arts have trickled down into the views of American youth.

The future of the liberal arts hinges in large part on the ability of people who share a passion for the liberal arts to be able to share their emotions with others. Seeing and hearing people who are fully committed to their art is often believed the best way of supporting the arts. The poet who intensely and emphatically reads his poetry reveals his commitment to his art; the philosopher who cleverly turns every statement into a question and undermines beliefs demonstrates the perennial and complex nature of philosophy; the novelist who convinces others to believe in her characters and care for their well-being shows the power of mimesis.

However, part of the current "terror" of the humanities is that these traditional ways of drawing people into the humanities are no longer working. Students facing the prospect of going into debt to attend college are less interested today in studying things that might be good for the mind, but are potentially hard on their wallets—and career aspirations. A generation or two ago, students were more passionate about things like poetry and history. The current generation though is more committed to pursuing lucrative vocational careers than enjoying the critical and creative wonders of the liberal arts, to relieving their massive student debt than pursuing majors that they believe will only exacerbate their economic woes.

Pollster Daniel Yankelovich has noted that "75 percent of high school seniors and 85 percent of their parents said college is important because it 'prepares students to get a better job and/or increases their earning potential.'"[11] In itself, the situation would not be so dire for the liberal arts if these students and their parents had some knowledge of—if not appreciation for—the liberal arts. After all, corporate employment aspirations (and success) are not mutually exclusive with an appreciation for the liberal arts. However, according to Yankelovich, "44 percent of students and 19 percent of their parents could not answer the question: What does a liberal arts education mean?"[12] In addition, Yankelovich's polling indicated that "[t]he overall impression of liberal arts education among 68 percent of the students and 59 percent of the parents was negative or neutral."[13]

These beliefs about higher education and its value would be challenges for the humanities even in good economic times. However, since the economic meltdown of 2008, they have made the situation in the humanities even worse. The rising cost of higher education and the shrinking job market coupled with prevailing perceptions about the value of a college education have had a decidedly negative impact on the liberal arts.

Some of the more disturbing numbers associated with this negative impact are the decreasing numbers of humanities majors. For example, forty years ago, 64,286 students received bachelor's degrees in English. However, in 2007, it was reported that the number of bachelor's degrees awarded in English had shrunk to 53,040. This drop would not be so significant if one did not also take into account that during this period, the total number of bachelor's degrees almost doubled. Taking this into account, the 64,286 majors in 1971 equates to approximately 128,500 in 2007, thus bringing the weighted decrease in English majors over this span to around 60 percent.[14]

Perhaps a better gauge of the state of the liberal arts though is the number of students who attended liberal arts colleges, but did not receive degrees in the liberal arts. In 1987, just over 10 percent of all students attending the 225 liberal arts colleges in the United States received degrees in vocational fields, whereas by 2008, that percentage rose to nearly 30 percent. At the lowest tier (or ranked) liberal arts colleges the percentage is well over 50 percent.[15]

Can the liberal arts get a bigger slap in the face than this? Is there no clearer indicator of the decreasing value of a liberal arts education than students attending liberal arts colleges but in increasing numbers *not* majoring in the liberal arts? In the same way that a drastic increase of business majors at colleges dedicated to the arts would not be a good sign for the arts, so too are increasing numbers of vocational majors at colleges dedicated to the liberal arts a bad sign for the liberal arts. One goes to Juilliard to study opera—not operations management; one goes to Williams to study philosophy—not finance.

Vocational aspirations and careerism among students are radically altering liberal arts education in America. The liberal arts curriculum is slowly giving way to vocational—or, if you will, *corporate*—instruction. If something is not done about this soon by critically engaged academics, there is every reason to believe that the move toward more vocational courses and majors will accelerate—and that the liberal arts curriculum that remains will more and more be tailored to serve the needs of an increasingly vocationally and corporately minded student base. How then do we as educators meet the demands of vocationally motivated undergraduate students while at the same time resisting emptying our liberal arts courses from their historical, political, and critical roots? How do we protect the distinctiveness of the liberal arts, while at the same time persuading students of their difference from vocationally grounded courses and majors?

CHAPTER 4

It is my belief that we need to not ignore the desires of our students or to denigrate them, but rather to engage them in a progressive form of dialogue with and through the liberal arts courses that we offer. "Corporatizing" literature courses does not mean that we ignore the historical and political dimensions of the works that we are teaching; rather it means that we need to be careful not to assume that students *prima facie* care about the critical foundations of texts. Teaching corporatized literature courses requires a more complex dialogue between teacher and students in order to respect mutual desires. In the end, however, this respect of different desires may be one of the only ways to prevent the eventual extinction of large swaths of the liberal arts curriculum—especially if our corporate liberal arts courses bring about a greater knowledge of and appreciation for the liberal arts.

Academics need to continue to show concern for the crisis in the humanities, but not by simply writing off its problems as intransigent or longstanding. Such responses only inflame fear and terror within the liberal arts—and are unproductive and unnecessary. Rather, by pursing micro-level adjustments in pedagogy such as the corporatization of liberal arts courses, academics can work toward altering negative neoliberal perceptions of the value of the liberal arts. Although most would probably rather teach their courses as "pure" liberal arts courses, this academic freedom is currently not widely available in the age of the neoliberal arts. So, until the neoliberal arts revert back to being the liberal arts, curricular compromises are one way to protect the liberal arts from immediate demise.

Terror in Academe

The primary emotional effect of neoliberalism in education is *fear*—if not *extreme* fear, that is, *terror*. Why? Because neoliberalism takes much academic decision-making out of the hands of academics and places it into the invisible hands of the market—and this terrifies academics. Absolute academic values such as academic freedom and tenure are rendered contingent under neoliberalism, which is to say, if professors no longer serve the requirements of the market, then they are rendered disposable, or if the fruits of scholarly deliberation are in conflict with the free-flow of the market, then they too are rejected. Moreover, the conjunction of neoliberal educational policy with the demands of a militarized state only exacerbates the fear in academe.

A neoliberal educational system gains much of its power through its control of academic emotions. It projects the state of mind in academe that at any moment one's academic way of life can be interrupted—or, if you will, terminated. "Terror is an emotion, a state of mind,"[16] writes George Lakoff. But, he adds, it is a state of mind that can be extended indefinitely. "Because extreme fear can be provoked at any time," comments Lakoff, "terror cannot be ended."[17] This means that neoliberal terror in academe gains its power by continuously projecting *possible* academic worlds unlike those we know and enjoy. If these possible academic worlds were ever to become real, then neoliberalism in education would lose much of its emotional impact on academics. Aristotle seems to confirm this later point in his description of how the emotion of terror works.

In his *Rhetoric*, Aristotle uses the term *phobos* for "a sort of pain or agitation derived from imagination of a future destructive or painful evil."[18] For him, the evil is always near at hand, and the persons threatened are ourselves. Often translated as "terror," Aristotle's *phobos* captures well the emotion felt by many academics today who are faced with the increasing neoliberalization of higher education. Few things in academic life are more painful than *imagining* academe without tenure or academic freedom. And many of us know firsthand the feeling of being a liberal arts scholar whose courses—if not department—do not *appear* to have a future in the neoliberal universe.

But again, note the emphasis on *imagination* in Aristotle's notion of *phobos*. Extreme fear for him involves thinking about a situation that is near at hand, but not *in hand*. The fall of the liberal arts *is about to occur*; the end of the university as we know it *is not far off*. Arguably, narratives that support these positions are key aspects of neoliberal educational power. The more academics believe that the end of academic life that they love and enjoy is just around the corner, the stronger the ability of neoliberalism to promote a controlling fear. It is a controlling fear that encourages compliance and compromise with neoliberal educational practices—compliance and compromise that can be as simple as "corporatizing" literature courses or as complicated as changing scholarly focus to avoid employment termination.

What is interesting is the way in which on this notion of terror allegedly "progressive" narratives about the university become agents of neoliberal terror in the academy. Without widely read narratives like Donoghue's, which project academic events like the end of tenure—or the professoriate—it would be much more difficult for neoliberalism in education to manufacture fear. The imagination, however, uses narratives like Donoghue's to motivate belief in a "future destructive or painful evil" regarding academic life—a belief that conveniently fuels the fear and terror that is arguably the warp and woof of neoliberal educational practice. The educational nightmare of neoliberalism is made even more intense when coupled with accounts by leading educational theorists asserting that change and reform in higher education are or should be slow. Take, for example, a recent work by Louis Menand.

In *The Marketplace of Ideas: Reform and Resistance in the American University*, Menand, a staff writer for *The New Yorker* who won the 2002 Pulitzer Prize in history for *The Metaphysical Club*, aims to answer four questions regarding American higher education today: (1) Why is a general education curriculum so difficult to institute? (2) What is the source of the "legitimation crisis" in the humanities? (3) Why do some people think that interdisciplinarity is so important? and

(4) Why do most professors tend to share similar political beliefs? In pursuing answers, Menand observes that "trying to reform the contemporary university is like trying to get on the Internet with a typewriter, or like trying to ride a horse to the mall."[19] In this regard, however, he is unlike Donoghue, who is simply content to rehearse the reasons why academia as we know it is about to end. Menand goes one step further and argues why reforming the aspects of higher education that do not work is next to impossible.

He reveals his hand early in the book in the following sentence: "I am in favor of reform when it shakes the system and not when it breaks the system."[20] Nevertheless, lest we despair that Menand's aims are not progressive, he follows this sentence with another: "I do think that intellectual life should involve taking chances."[21] It is interesting that Menand's book pays very little attention to telling us exactly what the "system" is. Although one would hope that it is more than Columbia, Harvard, and Yale Universities—the most frequently mentioned ones in the book—given the paltry range of schools (which are primarily Ivy League) discussed or mentioned in the book, there is little evidence that the system amounts to more than these and similar universities. Hard questions about the university system in America such as its elitism and its flawed logic of prestige and affiliation are not discussed. Nor are there many thoughts about reforming the American university system based on the educational needs and financial constraints of students—let alone the current negative emotional condition of academics.

Accounts like Menand's, which argue that reform in academe is—and should be—slow, have the unintended effect of providing the conditions for the continuous suspension of academic terror. If leading educational theorists and public intellectuals like Menand are suggesting that we should not make a radical break with the widely despised (but apparently longstanding) corporate university system, then the ability to promote fear and terror within academe gets a longer lease on life.

CHAPTER 4

Accounts of the emotional lives of academics are important windows to what works and does not work in academe. If collectively the main emotion that emerges from these accounts is extreme fear about their future within academe, then every effort should be made to eliminate the conditions that bring about that emotion. Narratives of the imminent demise of the university and the alleged inability of academics to do anything about it only play into neoliberalism's repressive structures—and make academic life more fearful than it needs to be. What is needed in hard educational times such as these are narratives that imagine academe beyond its despised and repressive structures—not additional accounts of future destructive or painful academic evils.

On Academic Terrorism

Terrorism is usually regarded as a form—and perhaps the most extreme form—of political violence. It is violence that is generally regarded as "unofficial" or "unauthorized" though always said to be in pursuit of some political end or ends. In many ways, it is commonly regarded as the paradigmatic form of political violence in a group of violent acts that include demonstrations, revolutions, and civil war. As such, for an event to count as terrorism, it needs to be not only a violent or intimidating action, but, more importantly, it needs to be unofficial or unauthorized. An authorized or official action using violence and intimidation in the pursuit of political aims is not terrorism but war. As an act of war, such an official action can count on indignation and an attempt at retaliation. The official warrant of an act of violence provides it with a comprehension of moral clarity that is denied the act of terrorism, or that terrorism, it might be more accurate to say, denies its target.

Regarded as such, the concept of terrorism seems remote to the everyday life of the academy. While the shooting of students at Virginia Tech, for example, may fit the received concept of terrorism, the emotional terror wrought upon academics by neoliberalism does not. Why? Because even though the emotional terror experienced by academics is intimidating to them, there is no physical violence associated with it. Nonetheless, there is something wrong with a concept that does not allow for the type of terror perpetrated by the presence of neoliberalism in academia to be considered terrorism. Perhaps at another time in history it would be reasonable to allow the non-inclusive concept of terrorism to stand. However, these are not "normal" times, particularly given their proximity to an historical event that has changed our understanding of "terror" and "terrorism," if not also many of the other terms through which we view the world.

Prior to September 11, 2001, "terror" was simply a state of mind, that is, an emotional state describable as being greatly frightened or being in a state of intense fear. However, after the attacks, terror became more than simply a mental state that most seek to avoid or to experience through artworks such as horror movies or tragic plays in an act of catharsis. Rather, it was *hypostatized* into something that exists—or persists—in the world. It became something with which we are at war.

To notice this transformation is to notice the way in which historical events can redefine and become disassociable with particular terms and concepts. For example, after the French Revolution, "liberty" became disassociable with this historical event in the same way that "holocaust" became indistinguishable from the genocidal events that occurred during World War II. Moreover, these major—or better yet extreme—historical events tend to reify terms and concepts. "Liberty," for example, became reified by the French Revolution in the same way "terror" has come to be reified as a consequence of the events of September 11, 2001. However, just because terms and concepts become reified or hypostatized by events does not mean that they provide any more insight on the event. In fact, as we know in the case of "holocaust," sometimes not even decades of reflection and response can solve the enigmas signified by the term. Nonetheless, reification is a sign of a basic change in the being of the term, or what the medieval philosopher Duns Scotus called its *haecceitas*.

In the weeks after the September 11, 2001, attacks, Jacques Derrida commented that received concepts like war, terror, and terrorism do not adequately account for what happened. In a way, the changes in their *haecceitas*—their *hereness* and *nowness*—facilitated by the events of September 11, 2001, call for a reconsideration of them. Writes Derrida,

> Such an "event" surely calls for a philosophical response. Better, a response that calls into question, at their most fundamental level, the most deep-seated conceptual presuppositions in philosophical discourse. The concepts with which this "event" has most often been described, named, categorized, are the products of a "dogmatic slumber" from which only a new philosophical reflection can awaken us, a reflection *on* philosophy, most notably on political philosophy and its heritage. The prevailing discourse, that of the media and of the official rhetoric, relies too readily on received concepts like "war" or "terrorism" (national or international).[22]

It is from within this space of "new philosophical reflection" awakened or brought about by the events of September 11, 2001, that the reconceptualization of terrorism is warranted.

Not only did the events of September 11, 2001, reawaken "reflection *on* philosophy" in America, they also called into question the very nature of the key concepts associated with these events. In the case of terror, the events of September 11, 2001, reclaimed this emotion from the realm of the aesthetic (viz., catharsis and the sublime), and pulled it back into the social and political realm. After 9/11, to speak of infliction of the emotion of terror is to call upon social and political thinking—if not also neoliberal thinking—rather than aesthetic feeling. As such, given the dominance of the emotion of terror within the academy, and a window in philosophical history open to rethinking the concept of terrorism, it seems appropriate to take the opportunity to imagine a concept of terrorism that accommodates both violent and (merely) intimidating acts of terror.[23]

One place to begin to motivate such a concept of terrorism is an article published more than thirty years ago by the philosopher Carl Wellman. In "On Terrorism Itself,"[24] Wellman avoids violence as a necessary condition of terrorism. Rather, he defines terrorism as "the use or attempted use of terror as a means of coercion."[25] In providing this definition, Wellman was well aware that it is much broader (and idiosyncratic) than most. However, Wellman believed that it "is illuminating just because it points to certain morally significant features that paradigm cases of terrorism share with other similar acts that fall outside the usual sphere of attention."[26] The academic terrorism promoted by neoliberalism would most definitely be one of the cases that falls outside the usual sphere of attention.

Though Wellman concedes that "[o]ne of the most effective ways of creating terror is by violent actions, both because such actions characteristically inflict great harm and because they inflict it in a striking manner,"[27] he is not willing to entertain violence as a necessary condition of terrorism. "When the terrorist engages in violence, this feature of his act becomes an important factor in our moral assessment of it," writes Wellman. "But the ethics of terrorism is not a mere footnote to the ethics of violence," continues Wellman, "because violence is not essential to terrorism and, in fact, most acts of terrorism are nonviolent."[28] An example he uses to motivate this atypical claim regarding the link between terrorism and violence is that of a "judge sentencing a condemned criminal to death."[29] This action on the part of the judge is considered by Wellman to be a type of terrorism "if he is deterring or attempting to deter potential criminals by using the terror of death innate in human nature."[30]

While Wellman's example of the use of deterrence in capital punishment cases as a form of (nonviolent) terrorism may seem far from the type of terror instilled by the practice of neoliberal educational policy (as there is no threat of death), his example of the classroom practice of threatening to flunk students is not. "I must confess," says Wellman, "that I often engage in nonviolent terrorism myself, for I often threaten to flunk any student who hands in his paper after the due date."[31] "Anyone who doubts that my acts are genuine instances of the coercive use of terror," continues Wellman, "is invited to observe the unwillingness of my students to hand in assigned papers on time in the absence of any such threat and the panic in my classroom when I issue my ultimatum."[32]

Wellman's example of classroom terrorism is not much different than the neoliberal administrator who threatens to cut faculty, courses, programs, and salaries, *if* neoliberal educational policies and values are not adhered to. It makes no difference to the neoliberal administrator that philosophy has been part of the academy since the days of Plato and Aristotle.[33] All that matters is that *if* students pursuing vocational majors are not interested in it, the program is expendable. On Wellman's view of terrorism, the threat of course and program elimination is clearly a form of terrorism—albeit a nonviolent form.

Efforts to "corporatize" liberal arts courses (such as described earlier in the case of literature courses) or programs (such as turning a Master's program in English into a writing or publishing program, viz., one that is vocationally aimed at training students to work in the publishing industry rather than disciplinarily based)[34] should be viewed as responses to academic terrorism: professors threatened with course and program elimination who "corporatize" them do so to protect themselves and their curricular areas from imminent destruction by neoliberal administrators. Corporatized liberal arts curricula, though the product of neoliberal coercion, still keep the hope alive that they will inspire new generations of students to pursue the liberal arts—even if the task becomes more difficult when the liberal arts are introduced with a neoliberal haze.

It is the use of *coercion*—not violence—that drives Wellman's notion of terrorism. "Coercion," says Wellman, "actual or attempted, is the essence of terrorism."[35] For him, terrorism requires three elements: (1) some terrifying or potentially terrifying action, (2) some future harm or evil ("though not the harm or evil of the past action that created the terror"[36]), and (3) the threat a harm will occur if the coercion is resisted. Academic terrorism in the context of neoliberalism fits squarely into Wellman's three-elements model: (1) the introduction of neoliberal educational policies into academe has been a terrifying action, (2) future harm to courses, programs, and faculty freedoms, and (3) termination of courses, programs, and faculty who resist *embracing* neoliberal changes. Under neoliberalism, academic tradition is no longer king; rather, whatever the market can validate takes academic precedence. In the case of the liberal arts, the coercion to vocationalize—or eliminate—them is a major political end of contemporary academic terrorism.

Wellman's concept of terrorism gives but one possible way to express the type of terrorism occurring in the academy. It is by no means the only way, nor is it not without its own difficulties. The point though of bringing it to our attention is to show one possible way to conceptualize how the kind of neoliberal terrorism now found in academe may be squared with the kind of terrorism where buildings are blown up and lives are lost. Both types of terrorism share the use of intimidation through terror, although one does this through violence and the other does not. While this may be uncomfortable to some political philosophers who require violence with their terrorism, it should come as comfort to those in academe who every day feel the coercion but have not been able to put a term to it. They can now call it what it is: academic terrorism.

Conclusion

The politics of academic emotions can reveal disturbing features of academe. The reality that most academics today work in fear of loss of academic freedom and tenure reveals fundamental problems with higher education today. The practice of altering courses and programs to avoid cancellation has become more common as an academic survival response to neoliberal educational practices. State and federal economic pressures and legislative mandates have only intensified the level of coercion in academe. The pursuit of knowledge should be a joyful event where one does not have to continuously look over one's shoulder in fear of saying or doing the wrong thing. To see terror as an emotion that pervades academe today is to recognize the degree to which higher education is in need of fundamental reform. To deny the possibility of reform is to extend indefinitely the current reign of terror in academe; to continue to present narratives (or "studies") of the academy that offer no exit to its neoliberal conditions is to subject it to a form of academic terrorism.

There has been and continues to be a blindness to the emotional lives of academics. The recognition that the emotional condition of many in higher education is best described as terror and that a notion of academic terrorism not only makes sense, but is probably more active in academe than many realize is very troubling. The events of September 11, 2001, have brought about an intense investigation as to the contemporary meaning of concepts like terror and terrorism. "[F]ear makes people inclined to deliberation," said Aristotle.[37] Academe must use this tragic historical window as an opportunity for revaluation and resistance to the destructive forces of neoliberal educational policies—and bring an end to the current emotional condition of the academy.

Conclusion

Twelve Theses on Education's Future in the Age of Neoliberalism and Terrorism

Jeffrey R. Di Leo, Henry A. Giroux, Sophia A. McClennen, and Kenneth J. Saltman

1. Neoliberalism is one of the greatest threats to the future of progressive education in the United States.

The goal of neoliberal education policies is not to improve education, but rather to increase the profits of private corporations. Profit-driven models for education directly contrast with the goals of progressive educators. The goal of progressive education is to educate students to be productive participants in democratic culture and to engage actively in critical citizenship. Such goals are not supported by neoliberal educational policy mainstays such as teaching to the test and standardized testing. Because neoliberal education policy tends to be data driven, it works against the development of a student's ability to think critically, thereby undermining the formative culture and values necessary for a democratic society. As long as the United States continues to view educational policy and practice through the lens of market-based values, there is little hope that progressive education, with its aim of educating students for critical citizenship and social and economic justice, will survive.

2. The war on terror and the discourse on terrorism have intensified the militarization of education.

The military–industrial complex should not be the driving force of education in the United States. However, the reaction to the tragic attacks of September 11, 2001, has become yet another excuse to allow the military–academic complex to drive U.S. educational policies, practices, and funding. Not only has funding been diverted from public education to support the war on terror, but there has also been a push to understand America and the world in a way that supports American imperial ambitions. The militarization of education encourages the rationalization of state-sanctioned violence as a social and political value and supports educational practices that validate this violence. The celebration of war as a sign of power and knowledge by the military–industrial complex obliterates the democratic values of equality, public debate of political problems, and respect for diversity. The militarized society eschews reasoned political resolutions to public problems in favor of eradication of the designated enemy/other. Hence, the war on terror is a war on democracy, difference, and thinking. Critical citizenship and democratic culture as the major goals of education cannot survive in a culture dominated by extreme fear and a war waged against an emotion, namely, terror.

3. The humanities are jeopardized by the rise of neoliberal educational policies and the discourse on terrorism.

Since 9/11 the humanities have suffered major defunding across institutions of higher learning. These cuts have been justified by arguments claiming the polemical (or biased) nature of humanities education—arguments aimed at questioning the value of humanities education. Consequently, the humanities have been the hardest hit among the disciplines in the defunding of higher education despite the fact that both the argument that humanities work is politically biased and that it offers students no value have been countered repeatedly by faculty and administrators. The impact of these cuts, though, has dire consequences for the development of a thriving democratic culture because humanities education teaches students the complex history of human interaction, conflict, and creativity while also encouraging students to develop their ability to critically analyze these developments. In short, the humanities teach students to read and write about the world, a skill that is ever more necessary in a moment of worldwide crisis. It is unsurprising, then, that the humanities have suffered since 9/11 and that there has been a neoliberal turn in higher education, because the humanities are the one place in higher education that can teach students to question the cult of the market and the military.

4. Cultural Studies has been a major target of the attacks on higher education.

One of the major disciplinary accomplishments of the past twenty years is the institutionalization of cultural studies in the academy. Areas of critical inquiry such as gender studies, race studies, sexuality studies, disability studies, and many others would not be possible were it not for the emergence in the 1990s of cultural studies as a disciplinary mainstay in the academy. Area studies allow interdisciplinary inquiry into the formation of a wide variety of aspects of culture. However, neoliberal imperialism has created barriers to cultural and area studies by encouraging uncritical defense of the United States as the global center of all that is good and allegedly democratic. As a result, emerging area studies such as Middle-Eastern studies have become appropriated by the military–industrial complexes such as the Department of Homeland Security, and foreign language studies are supported primarily on the basis of their ability to provide intelligence for government agencies.

Furthermore, the move by the state of Arizona to criminalize ethnic studies demonstrates the way that the neoliberal cult of the individual has worked in the post-9/11 atmosphere of xenophobic fear to deter the public from developing notions of solidarity and community. Arizona's HB 2281 prohibits any courses or classes that "advocate ethnic solidarity instead of the treatment of pupils as individuals." Thus the continuation of the discourse on terrorism and neoliberal educational policies threatens to severely curtail the development of cultural and area studies in the academy. As well, the application of market logic to all aspects of public and not-for-profit colleges and universities has resulted in the vocationalization of higher education, the direct involvement of corporations in designing programs, and the eradication of programs that are not seen as directly contributing to corporate profits and corporate jobs.

5. Educational innovation is not supported by neoliberal approaches to education.

Experimentation in the classroom is grounded in a critical pedagogy that values an open-ended, dialogical approach to education. The classroom in this vision of educational praxis is viewed as a potentially transgressive space wherein students and teacher mutually explore knowledge formations in a playful albeit critically engaged manner. Neoliberal approaches to educational practice shun innovation because these teaching practices attempt to foster autonomous, critically engaged citizens, rather than non-autonomous, fundamentally structured state subjects. Standardized testing, the centerpiece of neoliberal educational practice, is the enemy of educational innovation as are the neoliberal values of cultural isolationism and American exceptionalism. If the future of education involves the belief in and support for democratic culture, then neoliberal educational policies that are directed against educational innovation must be rejected. Technology on its own cannot be understood as providing social and educational innovation. As online learning technologies and educational social networking platforms are rapidly expanded in both K–12 and higher education these technologies must be used in ways that expand dialogic, critical pedagogical, and democratic values and social relations. Neoliberal approaches to education see such technologies primarily as sources of value—cutting teacher labor costs and expanding revenues regardless of the social, intellectual, and pedagogical effects of reckless technological expansion.

6. The U.S. public education system will be completely privatized if it continues to operate solely through market-based values.

The privatization of public education means more testing and less learning; more fundamentalist thinking and less critical inquiry; more vouchers and less understanding of education as a public good, and, ultimately, less investment in critical citizenship. If the push for privatization were based on evidence that it promotes a greater sense of civic engagement in students and supports critical inquiry, then the rejection of it would be much more controversial. However, it is based not on evidence but rather on the need to increase profits and support the educational-support-industry market. If the privatization of the public education system is not curtailed soon, there is a very good chance that critical citizenship and civic engagement as key values of the public education system will entirely disappear.

7. Education as a public good that prepares citizens for collective self-governance is compromised by neoliberal educational policies and the war on terror.

Neoliberalism and its formative culture of cruelty and militarization of everyday life, students, and faculty prepare students to support the military-industrial-academic complex. This goes against the notion that education is a public good that prepares citizens to engage in civic decision-making based on democratic principles. Market-based decision-making is less interested in citizens that are self-governing, and more interested in citizens as consumers who are corporately governed. The war on terror, through its attacks on academic freedom and threats to critical thinking, has made the academy into a site of closed—rather than open—inquiry. The result of neoliberal educational policies and discourse of terrorism is the loss of the university as a democratic public sphere in which intellectuals, educators, students, artists, labor unions, and other social actors and movements can form transnational alliances—as well as the loss of education as a public good.

8. The rise of neoliberalism and the discourse on terrorism bring about a denial of politics.

As higher education is vitally important to any notion of politics, the regulation and control of higher education by the military–industrial complex bring about the erosion of political activity, activism, and difference. The rise of neoliberalism and the discourse on terrorism have appropriated the political Left as much as the Right. This "denial of politics" and political difference paves the way for the rise of authoritarianism and the demise of dissent. It reduces citizens to predicable market forces and facilitates monstrous political subjectivities. In sum, the denial of politics in the rise of neoliberalism and the discourse on terrorism is also the denial of higher education as a progressive, political force.

9. Neoliberal educational policies in consort with the discourse of terrorism promote extreme fear among students and faculty regarding education's future.

The coming together of neoliberalism with the discourses of terrorism is particularly dangerous to education because it foregrounds the emotion of fear in the educational environment: fear of failing the test, fear of losing funding, fear of teaching the "wrong" topic, fear of saying the "wrong" thing, fear that the future of education is in jeopardy. It is not possible to freely and critically pursue knowledge in an environment permeated by fear. Learning and education should be joyful activities that bring about positive emotions. When the emotional environment of education foregrounds negative emotions like fear and terror, then it is not possible for progressive education to flourish. If the negative emotional environment established by neoliberalism and the discourse on terrorism is not reversed, it will be increasingly difficult to convince students and faculty that education is an emotionally satisfying endeavor.

10. Higher and public education are a public good and not simply a private right.

As part of a generational contract, education must be funded to promote programs and policies that contribute to and expand the common good and the social contract. Neoliberalism promotes education as a mode of training and focuses on technical training while undermining critical thinking and any vestige of knowledge that cannot be commodified, commercialized, and used to produce profits. Neoliberalism creates a culture based on values that enshrine privatization, commodification, the individualization of responsibility, and a survival of the fittest ethic. In contrast, higher education is a crucial democratic public sphere that provides the formative culture necessary to produce civic literacy and critically engaged citizens.

11. Governance structures in higher and public education should not mimic managerial models of corporations and market-driven organizations.

Governing structures should be democratized and organized so as to serve the constituencies they represent—including students, faculty, managers, administrators, and support staff—in ways that contribute to what is distinctive about an institution's commitment to democratic values, ideals, and social relations. This would suggest not only giving more power to faculty, students, and staff but also eliminating the casualization of academic labor.

12. Education requires public investment.

Higher and public education must be funded so as to reflect both a society's commitment to equal educational opportunities and its commitment to the deepening and expansion of a formative educational culture that creates the critical individual and social agents capable of governing a democratic society. This means investing less in war and more in education; it means making education free, especially to those who are marginalized by poverty. It means putting in place legislation and policies that tackle inequality in the United States so as to free American society from the casino capitalism that now corrupts politics and privileges a small percentage of the population.

Notes

Introduction

1. "College Access and Opportunity Act of 2005 or HR 609," February 8, 2005, Congressional Bill, House of Representatives, http://thomas.loc.gov/cgi-bin/query/F?c109:1:./temp/~c109Nk8yEy:e251.

2. "Education: A New Push to Privatize," Special Report, *Businessweek*, January 14, 2002.

3. For recent scholarship detailing educational privatization initiatives see Patricia Burch's *Hidden Markets: The New Education Privatization* (New York: Routledge, 2009). For the most thorough tracking of commercialism, see Alex Molnar's Schoolhouse Commercialism annual reports available at http://www.nepc.colorado.edu.

4. See Alex Molnar, Gary Miron, and Jessica Urschel, "Profiles of For-Profit Educational Management Organizations: Eleventh Annual Report," September 2009, Commercialism in Education Research Unit, http://epicpolicy.org/files/08-09%20profiles%20report.pdf.

5. See Kenneth J. Saltman, *Capitalizing on Disaster: Taking and Breaking Public Schools* (Boulder, CO: Paradigm Publishers, 2007) and Kenneth J. Saltman, *Schooling and the Politics of Disaster* (New York: Routledge, 2007).

6. For the clearest and most up-to-date coverage of the terrain and scope of public school privatization and commercialization, see Alex Molnar's annual reports on school commercialism online at the Educational Policy Studies Laboratory, http://www.school-commercialism.org, as well as Alex Molnar, *School Commercialism*

(New York: Routledge, 2005). See also Deron Boyles, ed., *Schools or Markets? Commercialism, Privatization and School-Business Partnerships* (New York: Lawrence Earlbaum and Associates, 2004); Joel Spring, *Educating the Consumer-Citizen* (New York: Lawrence Earlbaum and Associates, 2003); Alfie Kohn and Patrick Shannon, eds., *Education, Inc.* (Portsmouth, NH: Heinemann, 2002); and Kenneth Saltman's essay review of "Education, Inc." in the *Teachers College Record* (2003).

7. The majority of studies of charter school effects on academic achievement show on par to negative effects in comparison with traditional public schools. Two of the most extensive and significant studies were the 2004 NAEP results as analyzed by Lawrence Mishel, Martin Carnoy, Rebecca Jacobsen, and Richard Rothstein, *The Charter School Dust Up: Examining the Evidence on Enrollment and Achievement* (Washington, DC: Economic Policy Institute, 2005) and the Stanford CREDO study of 2009, *Disparities in Charter School Resources—The Influence of State Policy and Community*, http://credo.stanford.edu/reports/MULTIPLE_CHOICE_CREDO.pdf. Other studies include the following: Kara Finnigan, Nancy Adelman, Lee Anderson, Lynyonne Cotton, Mary Beth Donnelly, and Tiffany Price, *Evaluation of the Public Charter Schools Program: Final Report* (Washington, DC: US Department of Education, 2004); Helen F. Ladd and Robert Bifulco, "The Impacts of Charter Schools on Student Achievement: Evidence from North Carolina," Working Papers Series SAN04-01 (Durham, NC: Terry Sanford Institute of Public Policy at Duke University, 2004); and F. Howard Nelson, Bella Rosenberg, and Nancy Van Meter, *Charter School Achievement on the 2003 National Assessment of Educational Progress* (Washington, DC: American Federation of Teachers, 2004).

8. See Kenneth J. Saltman, *The Gift of Education: Public Education and Venture Philanthropy* (New York: Palgrave Macmillan, 2010).

9. See Linda Darling-Hammond, *The Flat World and Education* (New York: Teachers College Press, 2010).

10. Value-added assessment (VAA) seeks to measure how teacher practices affect test scores over time and then determine which educational methodologies result in higher scores. The approach has no way of dealing with the cultural politics of test content, how specific educational contexts might be the basis for critical or socially transformative learning. It more deeply entrenches the worst aspects of standardized testing, including radical empiricism and objectivism, which treat knowledge as something that comes from

nowhere and has no interests and values linked to it, and the denial of the inherently political dimensions of teaching and learning. VAA more deeply conceals the unequal distribution of life chances, naturalizing the unequal distribution of cultural capital as merit or natural ability as described by Pierre Bourdieu and Jean-Claude Passeron in *Reproduction in Education, Society and Culture* (London, UK: Sage Publications, 1977) with regard to testing.

11. Richard Lee Colvin, "Chapter 1: A New Generation of Philanthropists and Their Great Ambitions," in *With the Best of Intentions*, ed. Frederick Hess (Cambridge, MA: Harvard Education Press, 2005), p. 21.

12. Rick Cohen, "Strategic Grantmaking: Foundations and the School Privatization Movement," *National Committee for Responsive Philanthropy* (November 2007), p. 5, http://www.ncrp.org/index.php?option=com_ixxocart&Itemid=41&p=product&id=4&parent=3.

13. Andy Smarick, "The Turnaround Fallacy," *Education Next* 10.1 (2010).

14. This is detailed in Kenneth J. Saltman, *Capitalizing on Disaster*, Chapter 1. This is also taken up by Naomi Klein in *The Shock Doctrine* (New York: Metropolitan Books, 2007).

15. Paul Hill, Christine Campbell, David Menefee-Libey, Brianna Dusseault, Michael DeArmond, and Betheny Gross, *Portfolio School Districts for Big Cities: An Interim Report* (Seattle: Center on Reinventing Public Education at the University of Washington, 2009), http://www.crpe.org/cs/crpe/view/csr_pubs/295.

16. Ibid., p. 6.

17. The idea of taking advantage of disaster for radical market-based educational experimentation predated Hurricane Katrina in 2005, but that disaster was seized upon in mass media and policy circles to call for a radical market-based experiment in educational rebuilding. Paul Hill, who is the leading author advocating portfolio districts and its strategy of creative destruction, also authored an influential report with Jane Hannaway that called for refusing to rebuild the New Orleans public schools and instead putting in place privatized educational schemes. See Paul Hill and Jane Hannaway, *The Future of Public Education in New Orleans* (Washington, DC: The Urban Institute, 2006), http://www.urban.org/UploadedPDF/900913_public_education.pdf. This post-Katrina history is critically detailed in chapter 1 of Kenneth J. Saltman's

NOTES

Capitalizing on Disaster. It is also taken up by Naomi Klein in *The Shock Doctrine*.

18. For details of Hill's and the CRPE's spearheading of privatization under the urban portfolio model see Kenneth J. Saltman, *Urban School Decentralization and the Growth of Portfolio Districts* (Boulder, CO, and Tempe, AZ: Education and the Public Interest Center and Education Policy Research Unit, 2010), http://epicpolicy.org/publication/portfolio-districts.

19. Saltman, *Capitalizing on Disaster*, p. 32.

20. On the racialized discourse of discipline that infuses Edison Learning's pedagogy and curriculum see Kenneth J. Saltman, *The Edison School: Corporate Schooling and the Assault on Public Education* (New York: Routledge, 2005). Diane Ravitch celebrates the rigid approach of KIPP in *The Death and Life of the Great American School* (New York: Basic Books, 2010). Although Edison is a for-profit manager of public schools and KIPP is a nonprofit contractor, both shift the running of the schools to private parties and both target for takeover schools in predominantly poor and working-class minority communities. Ravitch admires the firm handshake and steady eye contact demanded of poor minority students, suggesting that such forms of physical control are the ticket to economic inclusion and academic success. Repeating a colonial educational trope and consistent with her nostalgia for pre–civil rights public education, this affirmation of corporeal coercion should be seen as centrally related to Ravitch's neoconservative view of culture that demands assimilation to a Eurocentric and conservative canon held to be of universal value and that allegedly represents the interests and histories of everyone. At the core of such an approach is submission and docility to powerful groups and institutions and their traditions rather than education as a practice of freedom and dissent in the critical pedagogical tradition.

21. Http://www2.ed.gov/pubs/NatAtRisk/index.html.

22. Http://www.whitehouse.gov/sites/default/files/rss.../national_security_strategy.pdf.

23. Stanley Kurtz, "Students Fight Back: Introducing NoIndoctrination.org," *National Review Online*, December 2, 2002, http://www.nationalreview.com/kurtz/kurtz120202.asp.

24. Some of the ideas expressed in the next two sections previously appeared in Sophia A. McClennen, "The Geopolitical War on U.S. Higher Education," *College Literature* 33.4 (Fall 2006): 43–75.

25. George W. Bush, "President Bush Announces Combat Operations in Iraq Have Ended," May 1, 2003, http://www.state.gov/p/nea/rls/rm/20203.htm.

26. The holiday was celebrated in the United States as early as the 1930s as Americanization Day. It became an official U.S. holiday in 1958 when President Eisenhower signed it into law under pressure from United States Senator Karl Mundt and Representative James E. Van Zandt.

27. George W. Bush, "Loyalty Day, 2003: A Proclamation," May 1, 2003, http://www.whitehouse.gov/news/releases/2003/04/print/20030430-26.html.

28. Ibid.

29. George W. Bush, "President Introduces History and Civic Education Initiatives," September 17, 2002, http://www.whitehouse.gov/news/releases/2002/09/20020917-1.html.

30. Even though we will refer to "the Right" as one cohesive entity, the Right is not one monolithic front, and the attacks on higher education stem from three different camps: the neoconservatives, who advocate a return to the traditional values of American society; the fundamentalists, who are interested in advancing their religious views in the classroom; and the neoliberals, who would like to privatize higher education by defunding all forms of public support and social services.

31. Hugh Gusterson, "The Weakest Link? Academic Dissent in the 'War on Terrorism,'" in *Dissent in Dangerous Times*, ed. Austin Sarat (Ann Arbor: University of Michigan Press, 2005), p. 84.

32. Jerry Martin and Anne Neal, *Restoring America's Legacy: The Challenge of Historical Literacy in the 21st Century* (2002), p. 1, http://www.goacta.org/publications/Reports/america%27s_legacy.pdf.

33. Quoted in Henry Giroux and Susan Searls Giroux, *Take Back Higher Education* (New York: Palgrave Macmillan, 2004), p. 29.

34. Ibid., p. 19. This quote appears from her co-authored book, *Take Back Higher Education*, written with Henry Giroux. In the preface, the authors claim primary authorship for certain chapters and the chapter in which this quote appears is attributed to Susan Searls Giroux.

35. Campus Watch, "About Campus Watch," http://www.campus-watch.org/about.php.

36. "National Defense Higher Education Act," 1958, http://ishi.lib.berkeley.edu/cshe/ndea/ndea.html.

37. Bruce Cumings, "Boundary Displacement: Area Studies and International Studies During and After the Cold War," in *Universities and Empire*, ed. Christopher Simpson (New York: The New Press, 1998), p. 173.

38. See Frances Stonor Saunders, *The Cultural Cold War: The CIA and the World of Arts and Letters* (New York: The New Press, 2000).

39. See Gene Wise, "'Paradigm Dramas' in American Studies: A Cultural and Institutional History of the Movement," in *Locating American Studies*, ed. Lucy Maddox (Baltimore: The Johns Hopkins University Press, 1999), p. 181, and Cumings, "Boundary Displacement," p. 163.

40. Quoted in Michael Bérubé, "American Studies without Exceptions," *PMLA* 118.1 (2003): 107.

41. Miyoshi 2002, op. cit., p. 40.

42. Ibid., p. 24.

43. See Sophia A. McClennen, "Inter-American Studies or Imperial American Studies," *Comparative American Studies* 3.4 (2005): 393–413.

44. See Paul A. Bové, "Can American Studies Be Area Studies?" in *Learning Places: The Afterlives of Area Studies*, ed. Masao Miyoshi and H. D. Harootunian (Durham, NC: Duke University Press, 2002), p. 212.

45. Ibid., p. 208.

46. Ibid.

47. Patrick J. Tiberi, "Opening Statement of Congressman Patrick J. Tiberi, Chairman," House of Representatives, Subcommittee on Select Education, Committee on Education and the Workforce, June 16, 2005, http://edworkforce.house.gov/markups/109th/sed/hr509/616st.htm.

48. Ibid.

49. Ibid.

50. Stanley Kurtz, "Testimony before the Subcommittee on Select Education, Committee on Education and the Workforce," U.S. House of Representatives, June 19, 2003, http://edworkforce.house.gov/hearings/108th/sed/titlevi61903/kurtz.htm.

51. "National Defense Higher Education Act."

52. "College Access and Opportunity Act of 2005 or HR 609."

53. Http://www.acenet.edu/e-newsletters/p2p/ACE_HEA_analysis_818.pdf, p. 8.

54. Http://firgoa.usc.es/drupal/node/46889.

55. The following summary of statistics on these cuts comes from the Consortium of Social Science Associations Washington Update: http://archive.constantcontact.com/fs021/1102766514430/archive/1105558801940.html.

56. Http://archive.constantcontact.com/fs021/1102766514430/archive/1105558801940.html.

Chapter 1

1. Hannah Arendt cited in Georges Didi-Huberman, *Images in Spite of All: Four Photographs from Auschwitz* (Chicago: University of Chicago Press, 2008), p. 31.

2. Zygmunt Bauman, *Collateral Damage: Social Inequalities in a Global Age* (London: Polity, 2011).

3. For an excellent study of the rise of military campus research in Canada, see *Operation Objection, Military Research in Our Universities* (Quebec: Anti-Recruitment Info, 2008), http://www.antirecrutement.info/files/Military%20research%20in%20universities%20-%20Operation%20Objection.pdf.

4. See, for example, Ron Jacobs, "A History of Repression—Cointelpro 101," *Dissident Voice* (October 9, 2010), http://dissidentvoice.org/2010/10/a-history-of-repression-cointelpro-101/.

5. Jeffrey Brainard, "U.S. Defense Secretary Asks Universities for New Cooperation," *Chronicle of Higher Education* (April 16, 2008), http://chronicle.com/news/article/4316/us-defense-secretary-asks-universities-for-new-cooperation.

6. David Price, "How the CIA Is Welcoming Itself Back onto American University Campuses: Silent Coup," *CounterPunch* (April 9–11, 2010), http://www.counterpunch.org/price04092010.html.

7. Nicholas Turse, "The Military-Academic Complex," *Counter Currents* (April 29, 2004), http://www.countercurrents.org/us-turse290404.htm.

8. David Price, "Obama's Classroom Spies," *CounterPunch* (June 23, 2009), http://www.counterpunch.org/price06232009.

9. Andrew J. Bacevich, *Washington Rules: America's Path to Permanent War* (New York: Metropolitan Books, 2010), pp. 17–18.

10. Kevin Baker, "We're in the Army Now: The G.O.P.'s Plan to Militarize Our Culture," *Harper's Magazine* (October 2003), p. 45.

11. Anup Sha, "World Military Spending," Global Issues Web site (May 6, 2012), http://www.globalissues.org/print/article/75.

12. Michael Geyer, "The Militarization of Europe, 1914–1945," in *The Militarization of the Western World*, ed. John R. Gillis (New Brunswick, NJ: Rutgers University Press, 1989), p. 79.

13. See, for instance, Loic Wacquant, *Punishing the Poor: The Neoliberal Government of Social Insecurity* (Durham, NC: Duke University Press, 2009); Jonathan Simon, *Governing through Crime: How the War on Crime Transformed American Democracy and Created a Culture of Fear* (New York: Oxford University Press, 2007); and Angela Y. Davis, *Abolition Democracy: Beyond Empire, Prisons, and Torture* (New York: Seven Stories Press, 2005).

14. Judd Legum, "House GOP Plays Ben Affleck Movie Clip to Rally Caucus," Think Progress (July 26, 2011), http://thinkprogress.org/politics/2011/07/26/280239/house-gop-plays-ben-affleck-movie-clip-to-rally-caucus-i-need-your-help-were-going-to-hurt-some-people/.

15. Susan Sontag, *On Photography* (New York: Picador, 1973).

16. Susan Sontag, *Regarding the Pain of Others* (New York: Farrar, Straus and Giroux, 2003).

17. Paul Virilio, *Art and Fear* (New York: Continuum, 2004), p. 28.

18. See Mark Reinhardt, "Picturing Violence: Aesthetics and the Anxiety of Critique," in *Beautiful Suffering*, ed. Mark Reinhardt, Holly Edwards, and Erina Duganne (Chicago: University of Chicago Press, 2007), p. 17.

19. This issue has been taken up in great detail in Henry A. Giroux's "Consuming Social Change: The United Colors of Benetton," a chapter in my *Disturbing Pleasures: Learning Popular Culture* (New York: Routledge, 1994), pp. 3–24.

20. Cited in Virilio, *Art and Fear*, p. 28.

21. Mark Featherstone, "The Hurt Locker: What Is the Death Drive?" *Sociology and Criminology at Keele University—Blogspot* (February 25, 2010), http://socandcrimatkeele.blogspot.com/2010/02/hurt-locker-what-is-death-drive.html.

22. Theodor Adorno, "Education after Auschwitz," *Critical Models: Interventions and Catchwords* (New York: Columbia University Press, 1998), pp. 191–204.

23. Ibid., p. 201.

24. Walter Benjamin, *Illuminations*, trans. Harry Zohn (New York: Schocken, 1969). See also Walter Benjamin, "Critique of Violence" in *Reflections: Essays, Aphorisms, Autobiographical Writings* (New York: Schocken Books, 1986).

25. Lutz Koepnick, "Aesthetic Politics Today—Walter Benjamin and Post-Fordist Culture," *Critical Theory—Current State and Future Prospects*, ed. Peter Uwe Hohendahl and Jaimey Fisher (New York: Berghahn Books, 2002), p. 95.

26. Ibid., p. 96. See also Susan Buck-Morss, "Aesthetics and Anaesthetics: Walter Benjamin's Artwork Essay Reconsidered," *October* 62 (Fall 1992): 3–41.

27. Sontag, *Regarding the Pain of Others*, p. 81.

28. Ibid.

29. Ibid.

30. Paul Gilroy, "'After the Love Has Gone': Bio-Politics and Ethepoetics in the Black Public Sphere," *Public Culture* 7:1 (1994): 58.

31. I take up in great detail the notion of a culture of cruelty in Henry A. Giroux's *Zombie Politics and Culture in the Age of Casino Capitalism* (New York: Peter Lang, 2011).

32. Geoffrey Hartman, "Public Memory and Its Discontents," *Raritan* 8:4 (Spring 1994): 25.

33. See, for example, A. O. Scott and Manohla Dargis, "Gosh, Sweetie, That's a Big Gun," *New York Times* (April 27, 2011), p. MT1.

34. The grotesque image can be found online at http://www.bjwinslow.com/albums/album90/Lady_Gaga_skeleton.jpg.

35. I have taken the term "poverty porn" from Gerry Mooney and Lynn Hancock, "Poverty Porn and the Broken Society," *Variant* 39/40 (Winter 2010), http://www.variant.org.uk/39_40texts/Variant39_40.html#L4.

36. Ibid.

37. Terry Eagleton, *The Ideology of the Aesthetic* (Cambridge, UK: Basil Blackwell, 1990), p. 344.

38. Zygmunt Bauman, *Life in Fragments* (Malden, MA: Blackwell, 1995), p. 149.

39. Ibid., pp. 149–150.

40. Sarah Lazare and Ryan Harvey, "WikiLeaks in Baghdad," *The Nation* (July 29, 2010), http://www.thenation.com/article/38034/wikileaks-baghdad.

41. Leo Lowenthal, "Atomization of Man," in *False Prophets: Studies in Authoritarianism* (New Brunswick, NJ: Transaction Books, 1987), p. 182.

42. Judith Butler touches on this issue in Judith Butler, *Precarious Life: The Powers of Mourning and Violence* (London, UK: Verso Press, 2004).

43. C. Wright Mills, "The Cultural Apparatus," in *The Politics of Truth: Selected Writings of C. Wright Mills* (New York: Oxford University Press, 2008), pp. 203–212.

44. Bauman, *Life in Fragments*, p. 151.

45. Reinhardt, "Picturing Violence," p. 21.

46. Mieke Bal, "The Pain of Images," in *Beautiful Suffering*, ed. Mark Reinhardt, Holly Edwards, and Erina Duganne (Chicago: University of Chicago Press, 2007), p. 107.

47. Ibid., p. 111.

48. Lawrence Grossberg, Personal Correspondence, June 18, 2011.

49. Eric Gorski, "45% of Students Don't Learn Much in College," *Huffington Post* (January 21, 2011), http://www.huffingtonpost.com/2011/01/18/45-of-students-don't-learn_n_810224.html. The study is taken from Richard Arum and Josipa Roksa, *Academically Adrift: Limited Learning on College Campuses* (Chicago: University of Chicago Press, 2011).

50. Tom Engelhardt, "An American World War: What to Watch for in 2010," *TruthOut.org* (January 3, 2010), http://www.truth-out.org/topstories/10410vh4. See also Andrew Bacevich, *The New American Militarism* (New York: Oxford University Press, 2005) and Chalmers Johnson, *Nemesis: The Last Days of the American Empire* (New York: Metropolitan Books, 2006).

51. Ian Angus, *Emergent Publics: An Essay on Social Movements and Democracy* (Winnipeg, Canada: Arbeiter Ring Publishing, 2001), p. 34.

52. Pacale-Anne Brault and Michael Naas, "Translator's Note," in Jean-Luc Nancy, *The Truth of Democracy* (New York: Fordham University Press, 2010), p. xi.

53. Georges Didi-Huberman, *Images in Spite of All: Four Photographs from Auschwitz*, trans. Shane B. Lillis (Chicago: University of Chicago Press, 2008), pp. 1–2.

54. Clare Hemmings, "Invoking Affect: Cultural Theory and the Ontological Turn," *Cultural Studies* 19.5 (September 2005): 557–558.

55. Zygmunt Bauman, *Does Ethics Have a Chance in a World of Consumers?* (Cambridge, MA: Harvard University Press, 2008). I have also taken up this theme in great detail in Henry A. Giroux, *Youth in a Suspect Society* (New York: Palgrave Macmillan, 2010).

56. Robert Reich, "The Attack on American Education," *Reader SupportedNews.org* (December 23, 2010), http://www.reader

supportednews.org/opinion2/299-190/4366-the-attack-on-american-education.

57. In personal correspondence, David Theo Goldberg spells out the nature of the cuts at the University of California system. He writes, "The projection for next year is a $500 million cut to the UC budget from previous state support of $3.3 billion or so (and an overall budget of $19 billion) for the system. About a $50 million cut to each of the campuses. And another $500 million unfunded mandate to pick up campus contributions to pensions. So we are looking at something like an overall 3–6 percent cut of [the] entire budget (including salaries and student support and all). Student fees have increased a total of 40 percent in past two years, though only those whose families earn more than $180,000 a year get to pay the full fees; those earning under somewhere in the vicinity of $80,000 a year pay no fees at all—so about half [of the] UC student population pay less than full fees. That said, [Governor Jerry] Brown has mandated that UC cannot raise fees again to deal with the next round of cuts—or else will lose further state funding proportionately. And where California goes often goes the rest of the nation."

58. Chalmers Johnson, *The Sorrows of Empire: Militarism, Secrecy, and the End of the Republic* (New York: Metropolitan Books, 2004), p. 291.

59. See Cary Nelson, "The National Security State," *Cultural Studies* 4.3 (2004): 357–361.

60. Frank Rich, "No One Is to Blame for Anything," *New York Times* (April 11, 2010), p. WK10.

61. David Price, *Weaponizing Anthropology: Social Science in Service of the Militarized State* (Petrolia, CA: AK Press, 2011); Chalmers Johnson, *Dismantling the American Empire* (New York: Metropolitan Books, 2011); and Bacevich, *The New American Militarism*.

62. Jacques Derrida cited in Michael Peters, "The Promise of Politics and Pedagogy in Derrida," *Review of Education/Pedagogy/Cultural Studies* (in press).

63. See Roger I. Simon, Mario DiPaolantoni, and Mark Clamen, "Remembrance as Praxis and the Ethics of the Inter Human," *Culture Machine* (October 24, 2004), http://culturemachine.tees.ac.uk/Cmach/Backissues/j1004/Articles/simon.htm.

64. Some excellent sources on neoliberalism are Pierre Bourdieu, *Acts of Resistance* (New York: Free Press, 1989); Noam Chomsky,

Profit over People: Neoliberalism and the Global Order (New York: Seven Stories Press, 1999); Zygmunt Bauman, *The Individualized Society* (London: Polity Press, 2001); Colin Leys, *Market Driven Politics* (London: Verso, 2001); Jean and John Comaroff, eds., *Millennial Capitalism and the Culture of Neoliberalism* (Chicago: University of Chicago Press, 2001); Doug Henwood, *After the New Economy* (New York: The New Press, 2003); Kevin Phillips, *Wealth and Democracy: A Political History of the American Rich* (New York: Broadway, 2003); Paul Krugman, *The Great Unraveling: Losing Our Way in the New Century* (New York: W. W. Norton, 2003); David Harvey, *The New Imperialism* (New York: Oxford University Press, 2003); Lisa Duggan, *The Twilight of Equality: Neoliberalism, Cultural Politics, and the Attack on Democracy* (Boston: Beacon Press, 2003); and Henry A. Giroux, *Against the Terror of Neoliberalism* (Boulder, CO: Paradigm Publishers, 2008).

65. P. W. Singer, *Corporate Warriors: The Rise of the Privatized Military Industry* (Ithaca, NY: Cornell University Press, 2008).

Chapter 2

1. Notable early exceptions to this include Frederick Hess's edited collection *With the Best of Intentions: How Philanthropy is Reshaping K–12 Education* (Cambridge, MA: Harvard Educational Publishing Group, 2005) from a neoliberal perspective, the liberal work of Janelle Scott such as "The Politics of Venture Philanthropy in Charter School Policy and Advocacy," *Educational Policy* 23.1 (2009): 106–136, and the work of Rick Cohen of the Center for Responsive Philanthropy. Mike and Susan Klonsky's book *Small Schools* (New York: Routledge, 2008) and Philip Kovacs's scholarship on Gates stand out as some of the rare critical work on venture philanthropy. See, for example, Philip Kovacs and H. K. Christie's "The Gates Foundation and the Future of U.S. Public Education: A Call for Scholars to Counter Misinformation Campaigns," *The Journal for Critical Education Policy Studies* 6.2 (December 2008).

2. See Robert Arnove's *Philanthropy and Cultural Imperialism: The Foundations at Home and Abroad* (Bloomington: Indiana University Press, 1982) and William Watkins's *The White Architects of Black Education* (New York: Teachers College Press, 2001).

3. For discussions of neoliberal education, see Kenneth J. Saltman's *Collateral Damage: Corporatizing Public Schools—A Threat to*

Democracy (Lanham, MD: Rowman and Littlefield, 2000); Robin Truth Goodman and Kenneth J. Saltman's *Strange Love, Or How We Learn to Stop Worrying and Love the Market* (Lanham, MD: Rowman and Littlefield, 2002); Henry A. Giroux's *The Terror of Neoliberalism: The New Authoritarianism and the Eclipse of Democracy* (Boulder, CO: Paradigm Publishers, 2004); and Michael Apple's *Educating the Right Way* (New York: Routledge, 2001).

4. See Kenneth J. Saltman's *Capitalizing on Disaster: Taking and Breaking Public Schools* (Boulder, CO: Paradigm Publishers, 2007) for a detailed account of the ways that neoliberal education has turned toward the pillage of public schooling and housing.

5. Stanley N. Katz, "Philanthropy's New Math," *The Chronicle of Higher Education* (2007), p. 2.

6. Ira Silver, "Disentangling Class from Philanthropy: The Double-edged Sword of Alternative Giving," *Critical Sociology* 33 (2007): 538.

7. These are discussed in Joan Roelofs's "Foundations and Collaboration," *Critical Sociology* 33 (2007): 479–504.

8. This history is discussed in Stephen J. Gould's *Ontogeny and Phylogeny* (Cambridge, MA: Belknap Press of Harvard University Press, 1985); Gail Bederman's *Manliness and Civilization: A Cultural History of Gender and Race in the United States, 1880–1917* (Chicago: University of Chicago Press, 1996); Nancy Lesko's *Act Your Age!* (New York: Routledge, 2001); and Enora R. Brown and Kenneth J. Saltman's *The Critical Middle School Reader* (New York: Routledge, 2005) (the last contains an exemplary excerpt from G. Stanley Hall's book *Adolescence*).

9. Georges Bataille, *The Accursed Share*, Vol. I (New York: Zone Books, 1991), p. 126.

10. The PBS mini-series documentary *The Triumph of the Nerds: The Rise of Accidental Empires* (1996) provides a valuable history of the early commodification of the software and computer industry.

11. David Harvey, *A Brief History of Neoliberalism* (Oxford: Oxford University Press, 2005).

12. Pierre Bourdieu, "Marginalia—Some Additional Notes on the Gift," in *The Logic of the Gift*, ed. Alan Shrift (New York: Routledge, 1992), p. 240.

13. The sections on venture philanthropy in this paper draw from Kenneth J. Saltman's *The Gift of Education: Public Education and Venture Philanthropy* (New York: Palgrave Macmillan, 2010).

NOTES

Chapter 3

1. Http://www.cnn.com/2008/POLITICS/09/26/debate.mississippi.transcript/.

2. Carl Schmitt, *Political Theology: Four Chapters on the Concept of Sovereignty*, trans. George D. Schwab (Chicago: University of Chicago Press, 2004).

3. Donald Pease, "The Global Homeland State: Bush's Biopolitical Settlement," *boundary 2* 30.3 (2003): 1–18. Amy Kaplan, "Where Is Guantanamo?" *American Quarterly* 57.3 (2005): 831–858.

4. Masao Miyoshi, "Ivory Tower in Escrow," in *Learning Places: The Afterlives of Area Studies*, ed. Masao Miyoshi and H. D. Harootunian (Durham, NC: Duke University Press, 2002), p. 41.

5. For more on these trends, see Henry Giroux and Susan Searls Giroux, *Take Back Higher Education* (New York: Palgrave Macmillan, 2004), and Sophia A. McClennen, "The Geopolitical War on U.S. Higher Education," *College Literature* 33.4 (2006): 43–75.

6. Henry Giroux, *The University in Chains: Confronting the Military-Industrial-Academic Complex* (Boulder, CO: Paradigm, 2007).

7. Stanley Fish, "Save the World on Your Own Time," *The Chronicle of Higher Education* (January 23, 2003), http://chronicle.com/jobs/2003/01/2003012301c.htm.

8. Stanley Fish, "Aim Low," *The Chronicle of Higher Education* (May 16, 2003), http://chronicle.com/jobs/2003/05/2003051601c.htm.

9. Sophia A. McClennen, "Neoliberalism and the Crisis of Intellectual Engagement," in *Academic Freedom in the Post-9/11 Era*, ed. Edward J. Carvalho and David B. Downing (New York: Palgrave Macmillan, 2010), pp. 203–213.

10. Naomi Klein, *The Shock Doctrine: The Rise of Disaster Capitalism* (New York: Metropolitan Books/Henry Holt, 2007).

11. Henry Giroux, *The Terror of Neoliberalism: Authoritarianism and the Eclipse of Democracy* (Boulder, CO: Paradigm, 2004) and Zygmunt Bauman, *Liquid Love: On the Frailty of Human Bonds* (Cambridge, UK: Polity Press, 2003).

12. Giorgio Agamben, *Homo Sacer: Sovereign Power and Bare Life*, trans. Daniel Heller-Roazen (Stanford: Stanford University Press, 1998).

13. Ibid., 9.

14. Donald E. Pease, *The New American Exceptionalism* (Minneapolis: University of Minnesota Press, 2009), p. 33.

15. Giorgio Agamben, *State of Exception*, trans. Kevin Attell (Chicago: The University of Chicago Press, 2005).

16. Henry Giroux, *Youth in a Suspect Society: Democracy or Disposability?* (New York: Palgrave Macmillan, 2009), pp. 7–8.

17. Henry Giroux, *Against the Terror of Neoliberalism: Politics Beyond the Age of Greed* (Boulder, CO: Paradigm, 2008), p. xxiii.

18. Ibid., p. xx.

19. Rudyard Kipling, "The Man Who Would Be King," in *The Man Who Would Be King and Other Stories* (New York: Oxford University Press, 2008), p. 247.

20. I developed some of these ideas about Afghanistan in a previously published essay "Reading Afghanistan post 9/11," in *The Impact of 9/11 on Arts, Entertainment, and the Media*, ed. Matthew Morgan (New York: Palgrave Macmillan, 2009), pp. 11–40.

21. Corinne Fowler, *Chasing Tales: Travel Writing, Journalism and the History of British Ideas about Afghanistan* (Amsterdam: Rodopi, 2007), 49.

22. Ben Macintyre, *The Man Who Would Be King: The First American in Afghanistan* (New York: Farrar, Straus, Giroux, 2004), p. 4.

23. Rudyard Kipling, "The Young British Soldier," http://www.everypoet.com/archive/poetry/Rudyard_Kipling/kipling_the_young_british_soldier.htm.

24. Ibid., 7.

25. Marc Luttrell, *Lone Survivor* (New York: Back Bay Books, 2007), pp. 9, 6, 10, 13.

26. Mahmood Mamdani, *Good Muslim, Bad Muslim* (New York: Pantheon Books, 2004), p. 18.

27. "War without Illusions," *The New York Times* (September 15, 2001), p. 22.

28. Fowler, *Chasing Tales*, p. 64.

29. Ross Benson, "The City of the Damned," *Daily Mail* (September 19, 2001), p. 11.

30. In an example of the first practice, Philip Caputo, who had lived in Afghanistan for a month, wrote for the *New York Times* in early October 2001 that "The mountains soar to 20,000 feet in the east, and endless deserts lie in the west." Philip Caputo, "20 Years of Training for War," *The New York Times* (October 4, 2001), p. 27. In an example of the second, Ben Macintyre wrote for the London

NOTES

Times that "Bloody war is sewn into the very land of Afghanistan, in the form of innumerable landmines." Ben Macintyre, "What Happens in Afghanistan, They Say, Decides the Course of History," *The Times* (September 15, 2001).

31. Mike Nichols, director, *Charlie Wilson's War* (Participant Productions, 2007).

32. These statistics come from Ann Jones, *Kabul in Winter* (New York: Picador, 2007), p. 214.

33. Khaled Hosseini, *The Kite Runner* (New York: Riverhead, 2003).

34. Latifa, *My Forbidden Face* (New York: Miramax, 2001). John Follain and Rita Cristofari, *Zoya's Story* (New York: Harper, 2003).

35. Meghan O'Rourke, "*The Kite Runner*: Do I Really Have to Read It?" *Slate.com*. Monday, July 25, 2005, http://www.slate.com/id/2123280.

36. Rachel Sandor, "Author Khaled Hosseini on *The Kite Runner*: The RT Interview," December 5, 2007, http://www.rottentomatoes.com/m/kite_runner/news/1690461/2/author_khaled_hosseini_on_the_kite_runner_the_rt_interview.

37. Ann Jones, *Kabul in Winter*.

38. Ibid., p. 242.

39. Ibid., p. 243.

Chapter 4

1. For an introduction to this topic, see my "Shame in Academe: On the Politics of Emotion in Academic Culture," in *Academe Degree Zero: Reconsidering the Politics of Higher Education* (Boulder, CO: Paradigm Publishers, 2010), pp. 33–42.

2. This is not to say that other emotions such as sadness, anger, and surprise are not a part of academic life. Rather, it is to say that a preponderance of joy rather than fear is preferable. If this is not the case, then the emotional condition of the academy is in very good shape—as fear is the dominant academic emotion today.

3. The American Association of University Professors (AAUP) is the foremost defender of faculty rights and privileges in America. Nelson, who has just completed six years as national president of the AAUP and is Jubilee Professor of Liberal Arts and Sciences at the University of Illinois at Urbana-Champaign, recently published

No University Is an Island: Saving Academic Freedom (New York: New York University Press, 2010). In addition, Ellen Schrecker, former editor of *Academe*, the official magazine of the AAUP, and professor of history at Yeshiva University, just published *The Lost Soul of Higher Education: Corporatization, the Assault on Academic Freedom, and the End of the American University* (New York: The New Press, 2010). Both books are excellent surveys of the assaults on academic freedom.

4. An abbreviated list also includes CUNY sociologist Stanley Aronowitz's *The Knowledge Factory: Dismantling the Corporate University and Creating True Higher Learning* (Boston: Beacon Press, 2001), and freelance journalist and New America Foundation fellow Jennifer Washburn's *University, Inc.: The Corporate Corruption of Higher Education* (New York: Basic Books, 2005).

5. Frank Donoghue, *The Last Professors: The Corporate University and the Fate of the Humanities* (New York: Fordham University Press, 2008), p. xi.

6. Ibid., p. xi.

7. Ibid., p. xv.

8. Ibid., p. 26.

9. One noteworthy recent exception to this trend is philosopher Mark Taylor's *Crisis on Campus: A Bold Plan for Reforming Our Colleges and Universities* (New York: Alfred A. Knopf, 2010). Taylor's book raised eyebrows with its argument that the university as we know it is outdated and broken, and requires nothing short of radical restructuring. Among Taylor's many suggestions for change are salary increases for productive faculty, and salary decreases for unproductive ones (p. 213); creation of a National Teaching Academy to support teaching excellence around the country (p. 190); and adding a fourth division for schools of arts and science called "Emerging Zones" in addition to the more traditional tripartite division of the natural sciences, social sciences, and arts and humanities (p. 145). His most controversial claim is to do away with tenure: "The only way for American higher education to remain competitive," writes Taylor, "is to abolish tenure and impose mandatory retirement at the age of seventy" (p. 204). Taylor, however, became a lightning rod for public remonstration because of his attacks on things like tenure and traditional disciplinary structures. One Barnard philosopher accused Taylor in the *Times* of "crass anti-intellectualism," while another critic in

The New Republic called his book "unbelievably misguided," and part of the growing "syndrome" of intellectuals turning incendiary, brief op-ed pieces into reckless books.

10. See Henry Giroux's essay in this volume, "Militarizing Higher Education, Neoliberalism's Culture of Depravity, and Democracy's Demise after 9/11."

11. Daniel Yankelovich's study is cited in Victor E. Ferrall, Jr., *Liberal Arts at the Brink* (Cambridge: Harvard University Press, 2011), p. 50.

12. Ibid.

13. Ibid.

14. Daniel Born, "What Is the Crisis in the Humanities?" *Common Review* (Spring 2010): 5.

15. Ferrall, Jr., *Liberal Arts at the Brink*, p. 55.

16. George Lakoff, "Beyond the War on Terror: Understanding Reflexive Thought," in *Transforming Terror: Remembering the Soul of the World*, ed. Karin Lofthus Carrington and Susan Griffin (Berkeley: University of California Press, 2011), p. 43.

17. Ibid.

18. Aristotle, *On Rhetoric*, trans. George A. Kennedy (New York: Oxford University Press, 1991), 1382a1.

19. Louis Menand, *The Marketplace of Ideas: Reform and Resistance in the American University* (New York: W. W. Norton and Company, 2010), p. 17.

20. Ibid., p. 20.

21. Ibid.

22. Giovanna Borradori, *Philosophy in a Time of Terror: Dialogues with Jürgen Habermas and Jacques Derrida* (Chicago: The University of Chicago Press, 2003), p. 100.

23. The foregoing thoughts on terrorism, 9/11, and conceptual change draw from Jeffrey R. Di Leo and Uppinder Mehan, "Theory Ground Zero: Terror, Theory, and the Humanities after 9/11" in *Terror, Theory, and the Humanities*, ed. Jeffrey R. Di Leo and Uppinder Mehan (Open Humanities Press, 2012).

24. Carl Wellman, "On Terrorism Itself," *The Journal of Value Inquiry* 13 (1979): 250–258.

25. Ibid., p. 250.

26. Ibid., p. 251.

27. Ibid.

28. Ibid.

29. Ibid.
30. Ibid., pp. 251–252.
31. Ibid., p. 252.
32. Ibid.
33. Proposed philosophy program eliminations at the University of Nevada–Las Vegas and Middlesex University (UK) are evidence of this. Both proposals for program elimination have drawn international responses against them.
34. Menand extends this comment though uses "nonliberal" rather than "neoliberal": "Almost any liberal arts field can be made nonliberal by turning it in the direction of some practical skill with which it is already associated. English departments can become writing programs, even publishing programs; pure mathematics can become applied mathematics, even engineering; sociology shades into social work; biology shades into medicine; political science and social theory lead to law and political administration; and so on. But conversely, and more importantly, any practical field can be made liberal simply by teaching it historically or theoretically" (Menand, *The Marketplace of Ideas*, p. 55).
35. Wellman, "On Terrorism Itself," p. 252.
36. Ibid., p. 253.
37. Aristotle, *Rhetoric,* 1383a14.

Index

Abu Ghraib prison, 44
academe, 115–116, 118–119, 120, 125, 127–128, 133–134, 139; *See also* academics; academy
academics, 24, 30, 38, 60–61, 97–98, 115, 119, 123–128; *See also* academe; academy; intellectuals
Academica, 5
Academies for American History and Civics, 31
academy, 115–116, 119–120, 124–128, 130–134, 137–138, 140; *See also* academe
activism, 69, 90, 140
Adequate Yearly Progress, 12
administrators: and emotion, 116, 120; and humanities work, 136–137; hiring of, 12; neoliberal, 132; relation facilitation, 116; supervision of, 29, 141–142
Adorno, Theodor, 47
aesthetics: and fascism, 47; of depravity, 42–43, 48–53, 56–58, 65; of disappearance, 44; conventional view of, 48
Affleck, Ben, 42
Afghanistan, 39, 54, 78, 100, 104–114; war in, 16, 33, 39, 46, 47, 65, 78, 100–101, 104, 108, 111, 112
Against the Terror of Neoliberalism (Giroux), 104
Agamben, Giorgio, 101–103, 104, 105
Agha Soltan, Neda, 61
al-Khateeb, Hamza Ali, 61

American Association of University Professors (AAUP), 117
American Comparative Literature Association (ACLA), 117
American Council of Trustees and Alumni (ACTA), 21
American Enterprise Institute (AEI), 7, 9, 11
American studies, 22–28, 96
Andrews, Lewis, 14
anti-Americanism, 22, 26
anti-intellectualism, 64–65, 67, 88
Apple Computer, Inc., 76–77
area studies, 22–28, 137–138
Arendt, Hannah, 36, 61
Aristotle, 125–126, 132, 134
Arnove, Robert, 70
Aronowitz, Stanley, 86
Arrighi, Giovanni, 81
artists, 3, 38, 65, 140
Auschwitz, 44–45, 47
authoritarianism, 104, 140

Bacevich, Andrew, 39, 63
Baker, Kevin, 39
Bal, Mieke, 57
bare life, 55, 94, 101–102, 106, 113
Bauman, Zygmunt, 53, 100
Benetton's United Colors Campaign, 44
Benjamin, Walter, 47–48
Bensons, Ross, 110
Biggest Loser, The (television show), 51
Bill and Melinda Gates Foundation, 6–7, 9, 67, 76

INDEX

Bin Laden, Osama, 49
biopolitics, 94, 95, 100, 103, 104, 108, 109
Bok, Derek, 118
Bourdieu, Pierre, 80–81, 92, 103–104
Bové, Paul, 26
Brief History of Neoliberalism, A (Harvey), 83
Broad, Eli, 7, 68; *See also* Broad Foundations
Broad Foundations, 7, 67
Bush, George H. W.: administration of, 71
Bush, George W., 17–20, 27; administration of, 31, 38, 41, 71, 81, 87
Business Roundtable, 68

Campus Watch, 22
careerism, 123
Carnegie, Andrew, 69, 70, 72, 73–77
Carnegie Corporation, 24, 70
capitalism, 15, 43, 73, 74–75, 81, 103, 106, 109, 142; disaster, 100, 103; free-market, 1, 100, 102–103; global, 25; neoliberal, 40, 55, 87, 100
Casey Foundation, 11
Center for American Progress, 9
Center on Reinventing Public Education (CRPE), 13–14
Charlie Wilson's War (movie), 100, 110–111, 112–113
charter, 4–8, 10–14, 68, 71, 87; schools, 6–7, 9, 10, 12–13, 16, 67–68, 71, 82, 87
Charter School Growth Fund, 7, 68
Cheney, Dick, 41
Cheney, Lynne, 21–22, 27
Chernobyl, 44
Chomsky, Noam, 104–105
Christie, Gov. Chris, 14, 32
Chronicle of Higher Education, The (Fish), 98
CIA, 23, 37, 38, 109, 110
Civic Education (program), 31
Clash of Civilizations (Huntington), 109
Clinton, Bill, 9; administration of, 71
Close-Up Fellowships program, 31
COINTELPRO, 37
cold war, 21, 23–26, 28–29
Cole, Juan, 38

Collateral Murder (video), 54
collectivism, 11
College Access and Opportunity Act (2005), 1, 23, 27
Columbia University, 127
Commercial Club of Chicago, 68
communism, 18, 24, 73, 75
Congress, U.S., 5, 23, 27, 29
Congress for Cultural Freedom, 23
Consortium of Social Science Associations, 31
consumerism, 80, 87–88
Cornell, Ezra, 73
corporate: aspirations, 122; capitalism, 51; culture, 67; economy, 76, 77, 84; exploitation, 90; fascism, 51; foundations, 68; globalization, 81; governance, 140; instruction, 123; interests, 32; jobs, 138; liberal arts, 124; media, 80; mentalities, 99; model of venture philanthropy, 7; online initiatives, 68; power, 32, 39, 40; rights, 113; sector, 5, 94; school reform, 11–13, 31, 82–83; taxes, 5–6; university, 116, 118, 120, 127; values, 119–120; wealth, 80
Creative Associates International Incorporated, 12
critical citizenship, 63–64, 135–136, 139
critical pedagogy, 138; *See also* pedagogy
critical studies, 121
critical thinking, 31, 39–40, 59, 140–141
critical theory, 43
criticism, 65, 96, 97
critique, 60–61; identity-based, 97; negative, 97; of nationalism, 96; social, 43, 98
culture, 21–22, 27, 41, 43, 49–50, 53, 55, 57, 63, 99, 109, 137; academic, 120; corporate, 67; democratic, 2, 4, 135, 136, 137, 138; educational, 142; foreign, 25, 28; formative, 32, 34, 36, 39, 40, 45, 51, 57, 60, 61, 64, 135, 141; German, 47; global, 25; inferior, 24; international, 20–21; military, 38; of cruelty, 3, 45, 47, 49, 50–52, 55, 58, 64–65, 139; of depravity, 3, 36, 41, 64; of fear, 1, 20, 32, 41, 65, 103, 136;

164

INDEX

of illiteracy, 60; of insecurity, 41; of neoliberalism, 81, 141; of peace, 66; of questioning, 65; of suspicion, 29; of war, 66; political, 104; popular, 63; screen, 39, 41, 46, 64; superior, 24; talk, 109; university, 116, 118; warriors, 25; wars, 17, 21, 24, 30; world, 25
cultural studies, 117, 137–138

Damrosch, David, 118
Darwin, Charles, 8, 45, 59, 64
death drive, 45–47, 49, 56–57
deconstruction, 97
democratic culture, 2, 4, 135, 136, 137, 138
democracy: and neoliberalism, 32–33; and protests, 32, 34; 32–33; classical, 101; devaluation of, 42, 79; future of, 58; global, 63, 65; ideals of, 34, 40, 60, 63; in the U.S., 1, 17, 34, 35, 60, 80–81, 102, 109; meaning of, 32; modern, 101; promotion of, 73, 104; substantive, 32; views of, 56, 59, 63; war on, 136
Department of Defense, U.S., 53, 80
Department of Education, U.S., 17, 31
Department of Homeland Security, 137
deregulation, 71–72, 80, 84–85, 89, 91; agenda, 67; ideology, 106; market, 49, 83, 103; of controls, 4, 87; public, 5, 32
Derrida, Jacques, 104–105, 130
developed world, 105
dialogue, 2, 15, 17, 57, 64–65, 91, 103, 124
Dickens, Charles, 32
Didi-Huberman, Georges, 61
disability studies, 137
Dobbs, Lou, 99
Donoghue, Frank, 119–120, 126–127
Duncan, Arne, 12, 30–31
DuPont, Pete, 10

Eagleton, Terry, 52
ecology: and anti-democratic approaches, 85; devastation, 88–89
economic dependence, 24
economism, 91

economy: bubble, 92; capitalist, 81; corporate, 76, 77, 84; consumer, 77; global, 87; global competition in, 17, 71, 84; global meltdown of, 33, 122; industrial, 77; knowledge, 17; market, 32, 49; of affect, 56; of desire, 47; of pleasure, 41, 42, 49, 51–52, 54–55; U.S., 71, 77, 86, 88, 90
Edison Learning, 5, 16
education, 2–3, 5–7, 11–13, 16–20, 28, 30–32, 34, 37–39, 56–57, 60, 63–66, 67–73, 76, 79, 84–96, 113, 122–124, 136, 138, 142; as a business, 5–6, 7, 10, 68, 115; as enforcement, 3, 15, 69, 78–81; assault on, 5, 8, 20–22, 26, 39, 62, 97; future of, 2, 4, 15, 141; higher, 1, 3, 19–22, 23, 25, 27–35, 36–37, 39–40, 58–63, 64–65, 86, 96–99, 114, 115–116, 119–122, 126–127, 134–142; influences on, 3; neoliberal, 8, 9, 11, 14–16, 40, 69, 71, 78, 88, 89, 116, 121, 125–126, 134, 135, 138–139; philanthropy, 7, 67, 69–71; policy, 1, 4, 9, 13, 21–22, 62, 69–71, 73, 83, 85, 88, 91–92, 116, 118, 125, 131–134, 135, 136, 138, 140, 141; privatization of, 7–10, 11, 13–14, 139; progressive, 1, 99, 135–136, 141; public, 4–16, 40, 62, 67–68, 70–71, 73, 76, 79–85, 89–90, 92–93, 136, 139–142; reform, 8–9, 12–15, 17, 31, 34–35, 69, 70–71, 72, 78, 81, 83–84, 85–88, 89, 91, 126–127, 134; terror, 99
Educational Management Organization (EMO), 5–6, 11, 82
Education as Enforcement: the Militarization and Corporatization of Schools (Saltman & Gabbard), 78–79, 80–81
egalitarianism, 87
Elementary and Secondary Education Act (ESEA), 6; *See also* No Child Left Behind (NCLB)
elitism, 127
emergency state, 26, 100
emotion, 47–48, 121, 125, 141; academic, 125, 133; of fear, 128, 140, 141; of terror, 125, 130, 134, 136, 141; politics of, 116

ethics: devaluation of, 42; different sense of, 61; and individualism, 45; of terrorism, 131; of violence, 131
ethnic studies, 138
Eurocentrism, 24
Europe, 34, 59, 62, 75, 109
exceptionalism: American, 21, 24–25, 101–103, 110, 138; assumptions of, 24; disaster, 3, 113
ExxonMobil, 68

faculty: and administrators, 116, 132; and emotions, 116, 119–120, 140–141; and humanities work, 136–137; as entrepreneurs, 33; contingent appointments, 116; freedoms, 133; in American studies, 24–25; in area studies, 24–26; research, 113–114; in international studies, 26; in neoliberal universities, 98; links to government, 29; militarization of, 3, 65, 139; post-9/11 suspicions of, 29; power and, 142; problems for, 120; public disdain and, 40; supervision of, 29, 114, 141–142; termination of, 133
fascism, 47–48, 51
FBI, 37
fear: as emotional effect, 3, 116, 124; controlling, 126; creation of, 126; culture of, 1, 20, 32, 41, 65, 103, 136; extreme, 124–126, 128, 136, 140; images of, 64; in academics, 133–134, 140–141; intensification of, 120, 124, 125; middle-class, 51; of change, 115; of critical dialogue, 64; of multiculturalism, 21; power of, 65; privatized, 65; promotion of, 41, 120–121, 126, 127, 140; reinforcement of, 50; spectacles of, 64; state of, 20, 23, 129 134, 141; vocabulary of, 54; xenophobic, 138
Featherstone, Mark, 46–47
Fish, Stanley, 98, 118
Fisher, Donald, 68
Ford Foundation, 24, 70
Fordham: Foundation, 7, 11, 68; Institute, 11
foreign policy, 38, 46, 94

formative culture, 32, 34, 36, 39, 40, 45, 51, 57, 60, 61, 64, 135, 141
Fowler, Corinne, 106, 109
Fox News, 51, 99
Foucault, Michel, 104
Franklin, Benjamin, 75–76
Freud, Sigmund, 45, 46–47
French Revolution, 129
Friedman, Milton, 73
Fulbright-Hays program, 31
Fulbright Scholar Program, 30
fundamentalism, 4; ideology of, 89, 130; market, 80, 91, 92, 104, 106, 113; religious, 63; rise of, 3, 109; shift toward, 24

Gabbard, David, 78
Gates, Bill, 10, 68–69, 76–77
gender studies, 137
geopolitics, 3, 21–22, 24, 94, 96, 98–100, 102, 105, 112
Gift of Education: Public Education and Venture Philanthropy (Saltman), 89
Giroux, Henry A., 3, 22, 30–31, 32, 97–98, 100, 103–104
globalization, 21, 25–26, 81
global studies, 27
Goldin, Nan, 57
Gospel of Wealth, The (Carnegie), 70, 73, 74
government policy, 41–42, 46, 66, 102, 113, 142
Great Game, The, 105
Grossberg, Lawrence, 58
Ground Zero, 96
Guantanamo Bay U.S. Naval Base, 96
Gusterson, Hugh, 20–21

Hancock, Lynn, 51
Hannah (movie), 50
Hall, G. Stanley, 73–74
Hardt, Michael, 104
Harvard University, 127
Harvey, David, 83
Hayek, Friedrich, 73
HB 2281 (State of Arizona), 138
Heartland School News (Heartland Institute), 14
hegemony, 25, 81

INDEX

Heidegger, Martin, 46–47
Henwood, Doug, 24
Heritage Foundation, 7, 68
Higher Education Act, 29–30
Hill, Paul T., 13–14
Hobbes, Thomas, 50–51
Holocaust, The, 47, 129
homeland security, 1, 27–28, 38, 100; department of, 137
Hoover Institution, 7, 11, 68, 73
Hopkins, Johns, 73
Hosseini, Khaled, 111–113
humanism, 120
humanities, the: challenges for, 122, 136–137; containment of, 119; crisis in, 124, 126; defense of, 119, 137; elimination of programs in, 30; field of, 30, 31, 117, 119, 121, 122, 137; organizations, 117; professors of, 117; funding, 121, 136–137; research, 97; terror and, 121; traditions in, 17; *See also* liberal arts
Hunger Games (movie), 50
Huntington, Samuel, 109
Hurt Locker, The (movie), 46

idealism, democratic, 39
ideology, 33–34; bias, 24; capitalism, 25; corporate, 76; deregulation, 106; educational obligation, 69; exceptionalism, 113; fundamentalism, 89, 130; militarization, 3, 38, 65; neoliberal, 8, 15, 21, 34, 59, 63, 71, 80, 92–93, 99, 103–104, 121, 131; of hardness, 41, 47; political, 8; privatization, 9–10; right-wing, 21; state of exception, 102; terrorism, 15
Imagine Schools, Inc., 5
imperialism, 101, 105, 107, 114; cultural, 24, 70; neoliberal, 3, 96, 98–99, 114, 137
individualism, 37, 45, 54, 55
infantilism, 54
Inglourious Basterds (movie), 50
Institute for International Public Policy, 31
instrumentalism, 60
intellectuals, 3, 35, 38, 65, 140; public, 61, 127; U.S., 19–20; Western European, 24; *See also* academics
Intelligence Community Scholarship Program, 37
International Advisory Board, 28–29
international studies, 21, 26–28
International Studies in Higher Education Act, 27
Iran, 61
Iraq: and militarization, 65; and troop levels, 78; and U.S. morality, 98; and video gamers as killers, 53–54; bombing in, 101; comparison to U.S., 46; cost and, 39; critics of war in, 38; influence on education, 19; post-invasion, 12; precedent of, 39; U.S. control of, 18; victims in, 54; war in, 16, 17–18, 33, 78, 100, 104
isolationism, 138

James, William (fictional character), 46–47
Javits Fellowship, 31
Javits Gifted and Talented program, 31
Jerry Springer Show, The (television show), 51
Jersey Shore, The (television show), 51
Jobs, Steve, 77
Johnson, Chalmers, 63
Jones, Ann, 113
Juilliard School, The, 123

K12, company, 5
Kabul, Afghanistan, 111, 113, *See also* Afghanistan
Kabul in Winter (Jones), 113
Kaplan, Amy, 96
Katrina, hurricane, 5, 12; effects of, 12–14
Katz, Stanley, 72
Killer Inside Me, The (movie), 50
Kipling, Rudyard, 105–108
Kirby, David, 44
Kirp, David, 118
Kissinger, Henry, 78
Kite Runner, The (Hosseini), 100, 111–113
Klein, Melanie, 47
Klein, Naomi, 100, 103
Knowledge is Power Program (KIPP), 16

167

Knowledge Universe, 6
Koepnick, Lutz, 48
Kurtz, Stanley, 17, 20, 28

Lady Gaga, 50
Lakoff, George, 125
language studies, 23, 27, 137
Last Professors: The Corporate University and the Fate of the University, The (Donoghue), 119
left (political), 140; critics, 72; curricula, 20–21, 30; educators, 98; -ism, campus, 17; on global economy, 87; progressive, 25
Leona Group, The, 5
Let Me In (movie), 50
liberal arts, the, 121–126, 132–133; *See also* humanities
Libya, 61
Lichtenstein, Jacqueline, 44–45
Limbaugh, Rush, 51
literary studies, 117–118
London School of Economics, 73
Lowenthal, Leo, 54
Luttrell, Marc, 108
Lynde and Harry F. Bradley Foundation, 10

Macintyre, Ben, 107
Mamdani, Mahmood, 109
managerialism, 82, 84–85
Manno, Bruno, 11
market: alternatives to, 8; competition, 6; costs, 40; deregulation of, 83, 89, 103; discipline, 15, 82; discourse on, 58; economy, 49; education and, 11, 68, 85, 86, 118, 124–125, 133, 137, 139; forces, 41, 140; free, 1, 94, 99, 100, 102, 103, 109; fundamentalism, 80, 91, 92, 104, 106, 113; global, 25, 27; growth of, 15; idealization of, 89; job, 117, 122; logic, 138; management of, 8; metaphor, 86; national, 7; new, 50; participation in, 113; positivism, 14; private, 7; public goods as, 80; rights of, 99; rules of, 106; self-regulating, 92; society, 32, 60; values, 33

Marketplace of Ideas: Reform and Resistance in the American University, The (Menand), 126–127
materialism, 37
Mbembe, Achille, 104
McCain, John, 94–95
McCarthy, Joseph, 23; era, 21
Menand, Louis, 126–127
Metaphysical Club, The (Menand), 126
Microsoft Corporation, 76–77, 92
Middle East, 22, 26, 59; studies, 22, 137
militarism, 16, 79, 81, 104
militarization: dangers of, 63; distinctive features of, 39; examples of, 16; forces of, 39, 62; ideology, 3, 38, 65; increase in, 1; of education, 3, 16, 40, 59–60, 65, 69, 78–79, 85, 99, 121, 136, 139; of faculty, 3, 65, 139; of society, 80, 85, 136; of U.S. security state, 81, 104, 125; opposition of, 63
Milken, Michael, 6
Mills, C. Wright, 55
Minerva Consortium, 38
Miyoshi, Masao, 24, 25, 97
Modern Language Association (MLA), 117
Mooney, Gerry, 51
Moral Collapse of the University: Professionalism, Purity, and Alienation, The (Wilshire), 117–118
moralism, 78
Mosaica, 5
movies: *See* terror
multiculturalism, 21
Musharraf, Pervez, 94–95
My Forbidden Face (Latifa), 111

National Commission on Excellence in Education, 16
National Defense Education Act (NDEA), 22–23, 28–29
National Heritage Academies, 5
nationalism, 96; post-, 25
national studies, 6
Nation at Risk, A (report), 16, 84
Negri, Antonio, 104
Nelson, Cary, 117

INDEX

neoliberal: agenda, 27, 30, 67, 69; assault on public education, 3, 5, 8, 40–41; capitalism, 40, 55, 87, 100; education, 7, 8, 9, 11, 14–17, 69, 71–72, 78, 80, 83–85, 89, 116, 121, 124–125, 126, 132, 134, 136–139; effects, 49, 52, 57, 58, 64–65, 70–71, 98, 100, 103, 113, 120–121, 124–125, 126, 132, 133, 136–139, 140–141; faculty research, 113–114; globalization, 20–21, 81; ideology, 8, 15, 21, 34, 59, 63, 71, 80, 92–93, 99, 103–104, 121, 131; logic, 3, 45, 73, 83; policy, 2, 3–4, 20, 54, 95, 116, 118–119, 125, 131–132, 133, 134, 135–136, 138, 139–140; privatization, 13, 14, 56–57, 67, 80; reform, 9, 15, 69, 72, 78, 83, 85–88, 89; values, 4, 54, 138; violence, 58–59

neoliberalism: and class, 69, 83; and culture of cruelty, 3, 50–51, 64–65, 139; and democracy, 32–33; and education, 1–3, 16, 65, 69, 116, 120–121, 124–126, 128–129, 133, 135–142; and ethics, 55; and pedagogy, 103–104; and racism, 65; and terrorism, 1-4, 16, 30, 64, 95–96, 99, 114, 131, 133, 140–141; and formative culture, 64; and the state, 16, 41, 80, 99, 106; biopolitics of, 94, 99, 113; birthplace of, 73; challenge of, 58, 60–61; culture of, 81; denial of politics, 17, 140; doctrine, 4, 94; effects of, 3, 100, 116, 124, 126; end of, 65; formation of, 58; ideology, 8, 80, 99; in the U.S., 25, 80–81, 99, 104; state of, 100; theory, 103

New American Exceptionalism, The (Pease), 102
New Schools Venture Fund, 7, 68
New Visions for Public Schools, 68
New Yorker, The, 126
Nichols, Mike, 110–111, *See Charlie Wilson's War* (movie)
Nixon, Richard: effects of administration, 25
No Child Left Behind (NCLB), 5–6, 9, 12, 82, 87; *See also* Elementary and Secondary Education Act (ESEA)

Occident, 107–108
Ohio State University, 119
On Rhetoric (Aristotle), 125
Obama, Barack, 9, 30–31, 94; administration of, 11, 17, 30, 32, 42, 66, 71, 81, 86
Operation Enduring Freedom, 108
Orient, 107–108
orientalism, 103, 106–109
O'Rourke, Meghan, 112
otherness, 55, 112

Pakistan, 16, 54, 94–95, 109, 111
Palin, Sarah, 51
patriotism, 26, 30–31, 38, 80
Pat Roberts Intelligence Scholars Program, 37
Pax Americana, 21
Pease, Donald, 96, 102
pedagogy, 8, 64; approaches, 15–16, 57, 124; critical, 138; cultural, 16, 65, 79–80, 85; militarized, 38, 40; model, 32; nature of, 63; opportunities of, 90; philanthropy and, 69; practices, 37, 64, 66, 90–91, 104; public, 41–42, 55, 61, 64, 91, 103–104; role of, 48, 57–58; state, 96; tools of, 61; values, 14, 139
Pell Grants, 62
Pentagon, 38, 40; attack of, 19
philanthropy: educational, 7, 67, 69–71; scientific, 69, 70, 72–73, 75–77; venture, 3, 9–10, 67–72, 77, 85–86, 89, 92
philosophy: nature of, 121; operational, 116; scholars, 118; study of, 117, 123, 130, 132
Plato, 132
Podesta, John, 9
policy: economic, 3–4, 32, 33, 45, 88, 95; educational, 1, 4, 9, 13, 21–22, 62, 69–71, 73, 83, 85, 88, 91–92, 116, 118, 125, 131–134, 135, 136, 138, 140, 141; foreign, 38, 46, 94; government, 41–42, 46, 66, 102, 113, 142; neoliberal, 2, 3–4, 20, 54, 65, 95, 116, 118–119, 125, 131–132, 133, 134, 135–136, 138, 139–140; privatization, 12, 85; state, 3, 26, 80, 102–103, 113
positivism, 14, 15, 85

post-colonial, 28
postmodern curricula, 21
poststructuralism, 97
pragmatism, 120; hyper-, 37
Price, David, 38, 63
Primer on America's Schools (Hoover Institution), 11
Professional Correctness: Literary Studies and Political Change (Fish), 118
progressive education, 1, 99, 135–136, 141; *See also* education
public education, 4–16, 40, 62, 67–68, 70–71, 73, 76, 79–85, 89–90, 92–93, 136, 139–142; *See also* education
public goods, 4, 9, 16, 55, 61, 80, 139–140
public sector, 8, 12, 33, 73, 76, 80, 89
public sphere, 3, 15, 32–33, 39–41, 56, 59, 63–65, 73, 91, 100, 103, 113, 141

race studies, 137
Race to the Top, 5, 9, 32, 82, 87
racism, 51, 65
Reading, Bill, 118
Reagan, Ronald: administration of, 16, 41, 71, 84
recapitulation, 74
Reich, Robert, 62
Reinhardt, Mark, 44
Renaissance 2010, 12, 68
Renner, Jeremy, 42, 46
repression: cold war, 24; government, 61, 81; military, 16, 80; of public education, 81; on foreign countries, 84; policies of, 118–119; state, 4, 16, 80, 96; structures of, 128
Rich, Frank, 62
right (political), 8; ambivalence to globalization, 25; and neoliberalism, 140; and public education, 10, 14; attack on faculty, 24; attack on higher education, 19–20, 21, 26, 30, 97–98; bullying, 33–34; culture warriors, 25; education policy, 21; extremists, 42; fundamentalism, 3; politicians, 32; privatization agendas, 68; rhetoric, 21, 27; support of charters, 8
Rockefeller Foundation, 24, 70
Rockefeller, John D., 72, 73

Roelofs, Joan, 70
rogue states, 55

sadism, 42, 45, 47
Said, Edward W., 26, 107–108, 109
Saltman, Kenneth, 32
Saw series (movies), 50
Schmitt, Carl, 95, 105
Scotus, Duns, 130
Scream 4 (movie), 50
Searls Giroux, Susan, 22
September 11, 2001: events of, 1, 15, 25, 27, 36, 41, 78, 81, 118, 129–130, 134; effects of, 1–3, 15–16, 18–23, 25–27, 29–31, 32–33, 38, 81, 95–101, 104, 106–111, 113–114, 116, 118, 120–121, 130, 134, 136–138; prior to, 31, 81, 96–97, 112–113, 129
sexuality studies, 137
Shakespeare, Einstein, and the Bottom Line (Kirp), 118
Simon, Roger, 64
Smarick, Andrew, 11–12
socialism, 73, 81
Sontag, Susan, 43–44, 48–49
Soviet Union, 23, 107, 110
sovereign: bare states, 106; country, 62; free market, 99; notion, 95; power, 94, 101–102; states, 99–100, 105, 108
Special Educational Service, 12
Sputnik I, 23
Stanford, Leland, 73
Stanford University, 73
State of Exception (Agamben), 103
students: and achievement, 6, 13, 71, 83, 86; and competition, 6, 82, 87; and emotion, 116, 120, 122, 140–141; and faculty, 98, 116, 117, 138; and funding, 23, 31, 60, 62, 83, 86; and knowledge, 8, 14–15, 17, 19–22, 30, 59, 82–83, 87, 90, 114, 121–122, 124, 135–139; and society, 89–90; and terrorism, 128–129, 131–132; as consumers, 8, 11, 33, 82, 85; as workers, 8, 122; brainwashing of, 26, 29; burdens of, 33; debt of, 121–122; goals, 91–92; graduate, 31, 132; in higher education, 62, 78, 119, 122–124,

127, 132, 135–139; management of, 5, 141–142; militarization of, 3, 16, 18–19, 21, 26, 27–28, 33, 37–38, 62, 63, 65, 79–80,139–140; of area studies, 26; protest, 24, 36–37, 58, 61–62, 66; special needs, 7
studies, 116, 118–121, 134; American, 22–28, 96; area, 22–28, 137–138; critical, 121; cultural, 117, 137–138; disability, 137; ethnic, 138; gender, 137; global, 27; international, 21, 26–28; language, 23, 27, 137; literary, 117–118; Middle East, 22, 137; national, 6; race, 137; sexuality, 137
Sucker Punch (movie), 50
Supplemental Educational Services (SES), 6
Supreme Court, U.S., 5
Syria, 61

Taliban, 106, 109, 111–112
Tea Party, 33
Teach For America (TFA), 7
terrorism, 1–4, 16, 100, 116; academic, 3–4, 99, 116–127, 129–134; and government, 18; and neoliberalism, 1–4, 16, 30, 64, 95–96, 99, 114, 131, 133, 140–141; and political violence, 128; and post-colonial theory, 28; and students, 128–129, 131–132; anti-, 104; as justification, 80; attacks of, 2, 20, 101, 112; concept of, 128–134; discourse on, 4, 15, 17, 136, 138, 140–141; ethics of, 131; examples of, 128–129; ideology, 15; nonviolent, 131–132; support of, 26
terror: and movies, 41–42, 129; and neoliberalism, 30, 64, 98–99, 125, 126; as a weapon, 30, 130–131; education, 99; -ist, 20, 26, 29, 100, 131; spectacle of, 63–65; state of, 54, 65, 99, 109, 113, 120–121, 124, 125–127, 129–131, 133–134, 136, 141; -think, 20; war on, 2–3, 15–16, 18–21, 25–27, 40–41, 95, 99, 136, 140
theory: bare life, 101; biopolitics, 104; critical, 43; cultural imperialism, 24; Darwinism, 8, 45, 59, 64; death drive, 45; developed world, 105; disaster capitalism, 103; economic dependence, 24; neoliberalism, 103; post-colonial, 28; recapitulation, 74; state of exception, 102; the sovereign, 95
Thurgood Marshall Legal Scholarships, 31
Tiberi, Patrick, 27
TINA (There Is No Alternative) theory, 8
Title VI, 23, 25, 27–31; Domestic Programs, 31; International Education and Foreign Language, 31; *See also* National Defense Education Act (NDEA)
Town, The (movie), 42
tribalism, 39, 110
Troops to Teachers program, 16, 17
Turse, Nicholas, 63

unions: labor, 3, 7, 12, 14, 30, 32–33, 51, 65, 72, 85, 91; teacher, 34, 87
Université de Montréal, 118
university: administration, 118–119; as public sphere, 3, 40, 65, 140; as "weak link", 21; campus atmosphere, 98; contemporary, 127; corporate, 116, 118, 120, 127; culture, 116; curricula, 20–21, 25, 115; demise of, 128; dimensions of, 117; faculty, 98, 115; funding, 30–31, 38, 62, 68, 73, 121; future of, 116, 126; militarization of, 38; non-profit, 138; programs, 29; public, 62, 138; role of, 37, 39–40, 73; scholars, 96; studies of, 118–119, 120, 126–127; students, 78
Universities in the Marketplace (Bok), 118
University in Chains, The (Giroux), 97–98
University in Ruins, The (Reading), 118
University of California, 62
University of Chicago, 73
University of Washington, 13
United States National Security Strategy (report), 17
Urban Institute, 13
Urban Portfolio: Districts, 5; Model, 13
USAID (United States Agency for International Development), 113

INDEX

USA Patriot Act, 80, 98

Vietnam War, 78
violence, 37, 42, 45–47, 50, 53, 56–57, 65, 131–132; acts of, 49, 61, 128, 131; aesthetics and, 43; alternatives to, 51; as intimidation, 133; desensitization to, 53; ethics of, 131; familiar, 53; high-intensity, 46; images of, 41, 51–52, 53; infatuation with, 42; market, 49, 64; mechanisms of, 40; neoliberal, 58–59, 88; organized, 37, 39; physical, 129; pleasure of, 52, 56; political, 128; production of, 40; real, 52, 53; representations of, 43, 44, 50; response to, 53; screen, 42; service of, 40; simulated, 52; spectacles of, 41, 42, 46, 48, 49, 50, 51, 56, 57, 63; staged, 53; state, 36, 41, 136; symbolic, 89; unfamiliar, 53; video game, 53; vocabulary of, 51
Virginia Tech shooting, 128
Virilio, Paul, 44, 48–49
vocational: careers, 122, 123; curriculum, 116, 123, 132; higher education, 138; instruction, 123; majors, 123, 132; training, 116
vouchers, 4–5, 10, 12, 14, 67–68, 82, 139
voyeurism, 43, 65

Walker, Gov. Scott, 14, 32, 34
Walton: Sam, 7, 68; Foundation, 67
Wellman, Carl, 131–133
We Scholars: Changing the Culture of the University (Damrosch), 118
We the People program, 31
White Hat Management, 5
WikiLeaks, 54
Williams College, 123
Wilshire, Bruce, 117–118
Wilson, Charlie, 110–111, *See also Charlie Wilson's War* (movie)
Wolin, Sheldon, 63
Women's Educational Equity program, 31
World War II, 129

xenophobia, 1, 138

Yale University, 127
Yankee Institute, 14
Yankelovich, Daniel, 122
YMCA, 74

Zelman v. Harris-Simmons (U.S. Supreme Court), 5
Zombieland (movie), 50
Zoya's Story (Follain & Cristofari), 111

About the Authors

Jeffrey R. Di Leo is Professor of English and Philosophy and Dean of the School of Arts and Sciences at the University of Houston–Victoria. He is editor and founder of the critical theory journal *symplokē*, editor and publisher of the *American Book Review*, and Executive Director of the Society for Critical Exchange. His most recent books include *Academe Degree Zero: Reconsidering the Politics of Higher Education* (Paradigm 2012) and *Federman's Fictions: Innovation, Theory, and the Holocaust* (2011).

Henry A. Giroux holds the Global TV Network Chair Professorship at McMaster University in the English and Cultural Studies Department. He has published numerous books and articles, and his most recent books include *Zombie Politics and Culture in the Age of Casino Capitalism* (2011), *On Critical Pedagogy* (2011), *Twilight of the Social: Resurgent Publics in the Age of Disposability* (Paradigm 2012), *Disposable Youth: Racialized Memories and the Culture of Cruelty* (2012), and *Youth in Revolt: Reclaiming a Democratic Future* (Paradigm 2012).

Sophia A. McClennen is Professor of International Affairs and Comparative Literature, and Women's Studies as well as the Director of the Center for Global Studies at Pennsylvania State University. Her books include *The Dialectics of Exile: Nation, Time, Language, and Space in Hispanic Literatures* (2004), *Ariel Dorfman: An Aesthetics of Hope* (2009), and *Colbert's America: Satire and Democracy* (2012).

Kenneth J. Saltman is Professor of Educational Policy Studies and Research at DePaul University. His interests include privatization of public education, militarization of schools and society, and globalization and education. His most recent books include

ABOUT THE AUTHORS

Capitalizing on Disaster: Taking and Breaking Public Schools (Paradigm 2007), *The Gift of Education: Public Education and Venture Philanthropy* (2010), *Education as Enforcement: The Militarization and Corporatization of Schools*, 2nd. ed. (2010), and *The Failure of Corporate School Reform* (Paradigm 2012).